Robert LaCosta's PORTALS TO HEAVEN is a very personal, yet universal exploration of memories, references, ideas, moments, thoughts, and much more to reveal inspired insights about God and every person. Robert has a fertile imagination and a deep love for God that will guide the user of PORTALS TO HEAVEN to see God all around them.
**Ted Baehr, Founder & Publisher, MOVIEGUIDE, Hollywood, CA**

What a great way to start my day. The Portal written so beautifully and honestly by Robert always makes me think, reflect, and know that we are all in this together as Christian brothers and sisters. Thank you Lord for your calling on my brother Robert and helping him show your face every day. And to remind us all to listen for the soft shuffle of your sandal feet.
**Butch Baker, Senior Vice President of Creative Services,**
**Hori Pro Entertainment Group, Nashville, TN**

Thanks, Robert LaCosta, for your inspirational, insightful, and often humorous devotions that encourage me to draw closer to Jesus Christ.
**Marlene Bagnull, Founder & Director**
**Greater Philadelphia Christian Writers Conference, Philadelphia, PA**

Robert LaCosta is an author with a crystal-clear voice. Reading his writing feels like we're having a conversation that helps me see the Portals to Heaven in my own daily life.
**Rob Brill, Religion Editor, Times Union, Albany, NY**

I know there are lots of devotional books on the market, but I can tell you that Robert LaCosta's devotional book is truly unique! It is a rare combination of theology yet highly practical when it comes to daily life. I have gained many great insights not only for walking with God but living it out as a result of this great devotional work! I highly recommend it!
**Frank Wray, Senior Pastor, Bethlehem Community Church, Delmar, NY**

I would like to thank you on the daily portals. These writings allow me to reflect on the many aspects of my life while giving me the opportunity to learn and read scripture relevant to that portal. I looked forward to reading these portals. They give me words of encouragement as well as thoughts for the soul. I also enjoy reading the response of others which provides me with a feeling of belonging, belonging to a community of people that encourage one another .
**Antoinette Renzi, Educator of the Developmentally Disabled, Guilderland, NY**

Bob LaCosta is a Holy Spirit gifted prophetic speaker and songwriter who brings the heart of God our Father to the heart of His children. Bob has profound insight that inspires, convicts, comforts and encourages in such a way that we are drawn closer and closer to knowing God's love and how to walk as His beloved children - representing Him in the world He so loves.
**Pastor Steve Lalor, Albany, NY**

# ROBERT J. LACOSTA

# PORTALS TO HEAVEN

*"Learning To Experience The Presence of God
through Metaphor-du-Jour"*

NO REPUTATION
COMMUNICATIONS

*Portals to Heaven*
*Experiencing God's Presence Through Metaphor-du-Jour*
© 2017 by Robert J. LaCosta

Published by No Reputation Communications, LLC. Selkirk, New York.

Layout and Design by Frank Romeo (First Impressionz)

# DEDICATION

To Father God, Jesus and The Holy Spirit who work so
tirelessly - and mostly effortlessly - to reveal The Holy Trinity
in - the - moment through metaphor, symbolism and analogy.

How can I thank You for sparing me from numbness?

May You be glorified
as You teach us to find You every day.

# ACKNOWLEDGEMENTS

I'd like to thank those family and friends too numerous to mention for their belief in and support of the writing and the reality of portals to heaven as expressed in blog form for many years. And to readers I may not know well or at all, thank you. It still amazes me that I can tap keys in America and have the result of that effort read on computers and mobile phones in India and beyond.

I'd like to give credit to Bethany Koehn who edited many of the portals and for her encouragement. Rob Brill, Religion Editor of The Times Union, was a player-coach in editing and a fountain pen of wisdom that could only have come from his years "on the desk." I would like to thank Jack Countryman for his wisdom and encouragement.

I would be remiss if I did not thank those whose study and teaching of the scriptures have helped me internalize The Word of God so much that it began to be impossible not to recognize God's presence in all of the metaphor-moments I refer to as "portals to heaven" within these pages and so many, many more that have either been private or not yet written.

Thanks go to Pastor Steve Lalor for his belief in me all of these years and Pastor Frank Wray whose daily responses to the blogs is the greatest compliment and encouragement a sheep of the fold could want.

Lastly, I would like to thank my wife, Vincenzina. I'm sure she has wondered what I've been doing these many years. I hope this humble work may give her a portal into the mysterious brain of her husband.

# INTRODUCTION

*PORTALS: An entrance or gateway.*

*Portals to Heaven: The deliberate effort to observe actual and metaphorical glimpses and realities of heaven in everyday life and to respond accordingly.*

Experiencing the presence of God in the now and in the moment and in the every day is not like practicing the piano with Mom leaning over your shoulder.

It's the most joyful journey you'll ever take.

It's a deliberate effort to look beyond this world and see what God is showing you *from* heaven. I call this Portals to Heaven rather than from heaven because it is from our perspective. But I acknowledge that you could use both interchangeably in some respect.

Portals to Heaven are not reserved for some crowning moments, an intense sermon, a lovely song of worship, a walk down the aisle or a graduation ceremony.

They are for right now.

Jesus had this communion down. He said, "I do only what I see the Father do." It's a constant thing.

It may seem overwhelming, but it's not. When your mind and heart become alert to these clues and cues and begin experiencing this deliberate choice to walk on earth as it is in heaven, the Portals to Heaven will become the norm and not the exception.

Used as a working devotional, Portals to Heaven will give you plenty of these examples with accompanying scriptures that match the metaphor. They will help you learn to observe the array of portals that surround you.

I have begun to pick up on these hints of heaven and foretastes of eternity through observation, a little discipline and, well … practice.

Whether subtle or obvious, God is showing me that it's a little bit like hide 'n' seek or a scavenger hunt because he has made these portals so accessible. That's where the joy comes in.

I have spotted this presence of God in funeral parlors. I have noticed it in my funny bones. From the sublime to the ridiculous, God had always planned this path of life to be one that is wide enough for two. Pain and laughter, joy and sorrow and everything in between can be portals with a little practice.

I sometimes write in the first person because these are portals I witness. I know you will relate to most or all of them. But I want you to begin to see Portals of heaven in the *now* and journal in the first person with The First Person.

That is why each week's portal has a blank page. Write or draw the portals you see as you experience them. They do not have to match that particular week's topic. In fact, they probably won't. I don't want you necessarily seeing portals that I see. You need to experience God through the portals He is showing you.


Happy portaling,

Robert J. LaCosta

(a.k.a. Beloved Blogger)

# January

# February

# March

# April

# May

# June

# July

# August

# September

# October

# November

# December

# January
## PORTALS TO HEAVEN

Our senses provide great portals.

As a hearing instrument specialist, I have had the honor of witnessing the world of sound open up for patients whose world had grown silent. It's quite a privilege. It's also showed me how critical this sense can be to relationships.

One woman who came in for a hearing test had other physical maladies as well as the hearing loss. She had just come from watching her neighbor's cats. As a test, I suggested that her accompanying husband ask her an unexpected question that so that I could observe how the loss was affecting her life.

"Are you getting the cats again?" he innocently asked. Her face grew red with anger and she barked, "Am I getting a CAT scan? You didn't even tell me the doctor ordered one!"

After I prevented her from punching the poor guy, I fit her with hearing aids that might have saved their marriage.

The most common hearing loss is from aging. It's insidious because the patient and the family perceive it gradually. It progresses from being an annoyance to a daily argument.

## ℘ORTAL ℧O ℋEAVEN

The hearing impaired can get assistance and it's the same in the supernatural. The Holy Spirit becomes our "aid" to hear God's Word through scripture, personal encouragement and direction.

*Incline your ear, and come to me; hear, that your soul may live…Guard your heart above all else, for it determines the course of your life…whatever he hears he will speak…Do not stifle the Holy Spirit.*

**Isaiah 55:3 (ESV), Proverbs 4:23 (NLT), John 16:13 (NASB),**
**1 Thessalonians 5:19 (NLT)**

*Touch* is one of our five senses and it can have a great impact on what we perceive – as in "on earth as it is in heaven." During just one day, I touched and was touched…

Following an extremely brief gravesite memorial service after a long drive, I was wondering if our presence had made a difference to the grieving heart of our friend.

"Seeing you made my day," she said through tears and a lengthy hug in the middle of the cemetery. We touched her.

Later, an interview turned into an opportunity to befriend this senior citizen. During our talk, he mentioned that he had always been fascinated with trains but had only been on one in his entire life. We made a date to go on a train ride together.

It touched him.

I was a bit weary later in the day when I walked into a large stationary supply store. A thoughtful worker rushed to open up her register seeing me in a long line. She also patiently explained why my rewards card had mysteriously disappeared two years ago and reinstated my account. On my way out, the store manager stopped and offered some advice about a sign that piqued my interest. Neither knew of my weariness. They touched me.

## ᏢORTAL ᏁTO ᏧᎬAVEN

Our Father is always looking to touch - whether we are
the ones being used or receiving.

---

*Then He touched the [blind men's] eyes, saying, 'According to your faith let it be to you.' And their eyes were opened… But when He saw the multitudes, He was moved with compassion for them, because they were weary and scattered, like sheep having no shepherd.*

**Matthew 9:29,36 (NKJV). Editor's brackets. Also read: Matthew 8:3,14 (NKJV)**

Olfactory pleasantries and warnings are two sides of a coin.

Nature provides indescribable delights through flowers. Few things are more pleasant to the senses than walking down a path lined with honeysuckles. Such evidence of God could turn an atheist into a believer before the end of his walk.

There is another side to scents. Those who have been on mission trips know when they are near open sewerage areas. A World War II vet who helped liberate concentration camps disclosed that no one forgets the overpowering smell of death. If our spirits are unguarded, some of those odors could turn a believer into an atheist.

And then there are those who have had near-death experiences that testify that heaven wafts with fragrances beyond the pale.

On earth, the tiniest of flowers can arrest our senses though we can't see what's doing the arresting.

## PORTAL TO HEAVEN

God puts these juxtaposing fragrances and odors to symbolize good and bad. We get to choose. St. Paul says that our love for others is the aroma that stops people in their tracks no matter what path they take. In short, we are to be heaven-scent.

*For we are a fragrance of Christ to God among those who are being saved and among those who are perishing… Therefore be imitators of God, as beloved children; and walk in love, just as Christ also loved you and gave Himself up for us, an offering and a sacrifice to God as a fragrant aroma.*

**2 Corinthians 2:15 (NASB), Ephesians 5:1,2 (NASB)**

My tastes are that of a simple man. That doesn't mean I think that others shouldn't enjoy the nuances of food, culture, cars, sports and other goodies of life.

I've been involved in conversations about elaborate recipes and subtle spices, the emotional state of the composer 300 years ago, the intricacies of a carburetor or the specific training methods of zoned-athletes. If you know every line in a movie, good for you. I can, on certain days, remember how to spell my name. Why in the world would God make us so different?

He is trying to make it clear that He has a very specific interest in us. For those who have recognized Him as their Master Chef, He will use each one in His carefully complex concoction.

## ᴘORTAL ᴄᴛO ꜰꜰEAVEN

Recipes are used in corner-store sandwich shops, chains, mom'n pop luncheonettes, diners and gourmet restaurants. Even simple guys like me might be made into a good grilled cheese. God is using His dishes to tempt the taste buds of the unbeliever no matter where we are served. As simply complicated as that sounds, it's the mark of The Chef with good taste.

*O taste and see that the LORD is good… if you have tasted the kindness of the Lord… How sweet are Your words to my taste! Yes, sweeter than honey to my mouth… Your words were found and I ate them, And Your words became for me a joy and the delight of my heart; For I have been called by Your name, O LORD God of hosts.*

**Psalm 34:8 (KJV), 1 Peter 2:3 (NASB), Psalm 119:103 (NASB), Jeremiah 15:16 (NASB)**

I'm walking in a beautiful art gallery and there's a long hallway leading to a painting that I am drawn to and yet it seems just out of sight. Suddenly, this portrait of Christ comes into stunning clarity. I gaze. I understand all. I weep. And there's a power shortage…

Dreams like this have a way of waking us up. There are times when we see Jesus come into view and then boom! Some darkness in our soul or some circumstance blocks our gaze and we feel as though we are back to square one. Sometimes the dark comes over time and hides the details of the face of Christ the way the centuries of candle-soot hid the brightness and clarity of the paintings on the ceiling of The Sistine Chapel.

Light makes everything come into view.

In the spiritual realm, those words in red in The New Testament seem to be the flashlight that The Holy Spirit is holding for us. Unlike our natural eyes that dim with age, Christ has promised that we will see better the closer we get to the hallways of heaven.

St. John says we are going to be a mirror-image of Christ because we will see Him exactly as He is and it will be impossible to be anything but a perfect reproduction of the portrait of Christ.

## ᏒORTAL ᎢO ᎻEAVEN

There are many portraits of Christ in the gallery of life that will come alive to the wakeful eye.

*Therefore we do not lose heart. Though outwardly we are wasting away, yet inwardly we are being renewed day by day… For now we see in a mirror, dimly, but then face to face 2 Corinthians 4:16*

**(NIV), 1 Corinthians 13:12, (NKJV) Also read: 1 John 3:2 (ISV)**

direction + truth    2 Cor 4:16  ∴ we do
not lose heart. Though outwardly we are
wasting away, yet inwardly we are being
renewed day by day. For our light and
momentary troubles are achieving for
us an eternal glory that far outweighs
them all. So we fix our eyes not on
what is seen, but on what is unseen.
For what is seen is temporary, but
what is unseen is eternal.

Scrooge should be the poster child for New Year's Resolutions.

Truly, repentance is the best way to start the calendar year. Sin is a terrible weight and we really can't go anywhere carrying the heavy bags of guilt. Repentance is simply the honor and reality of telling God, "You are perfect and it's clear that I am not."

Yet, the genius of this classic by Charles Dickens is in the irony that Scrooge goes through the longest night and yet the shortest route to repentance. The reason Scrooge is a favorite is because he represents everyone. We are all the reluctant repentant. On every page, Scrooge is either complaining that he can't change or that he is the same as everyone else or that he is too old.

This reluctant repentant desires to change…but not so fast! Like us, he wants the effects of repentance overnight.

When Scrooge gives in, clings to the Ghost of Christmas Future and says, "I do repent, I do repent, I am not the man I was," we all love it and simultaneously wish it was that easy for us.

## ᏢORTAL ᏟᎢO ᎻEAVEN

Whether easy or not, short or long, repentance is worth every inch of our pride slipping away. Someone snap a picture of Scrooge for the New Year's Resolution poster.

*Therefore repent and return, so that your sins may be wiped away, in order that times of refreshing may come from the presence of the Lord.*

**Acts 3:19 (NASB)**

"Clear The Calendar!"

What if one were to look at that calendar square of January 1 as a fantastic, incredible, monumental time to…repent? "Wet blanket" might be the response. Yet, think of the possibilities.

Some might be scared of repentance for any number of reasons. Looking up to God or in a mirror and admitting to faults or weaknesses can be frightening.

As if that isn't enough, going to others and telling them what you just told God and your mirror can be terrifying. It can also be amazingly freeing.

We don't keep up old calendars. They are unnecessary and block the view of the new calendar that contains all of those nice, white and CLEAR blocks that represent all sorts of potential.

## ᴘORTAL ᴛO ᕼEAVEN

Clear the air. You'll be able to read the calendar better, see the mirror and have a much better view of God's forgiveness and His grace-filled face. Looking at our weaknesses is simply a humble ways of saying, "We're all human" without dismissing our need for repentance. We all know how long a year can be so why make it any longer?

*Come close to God, and he will come close to you. Clean up your lives, you sinners, and CLEAR your minds, you doubters…Confess your sins to each other and pray for each other so that you may be healed…Now we see a blurred image in a mirror. Then we will see very clearly.*

**James 4:8 (GWT), James 5:16 (NLT), 1Corinthians 13:12 (GWT)**

Sometimes what is drilled into our heads takes a lot of time and practice to get undrilled.

It starts when we are young. You've either accidentally or intentionally let the dog off its line, and you and your buddy agree to show your mom a blank face when she asks you why she's not hearing the dog bark.

Later in life, a lawyer tells you that you must never admit to guilt whether it's a simple speeding ticket, a fender bender, or something worse.

Pleading "Not guilty" when we know we are is perhaps the greatest proof of God's existence and holiness. The guilty conscience assures us we are not right with someone; and that someone is God.

We must remember He's been hearing this bull since Adam and Eve's creative version of what transpired in the Garden of Eden.

In the courtroom of heaven He asks us to approach the bench and whispers, "Now what really happened?" We shouldn't be surprised at the smirk on His face.

## PORTAL TO HEAVEN

There is utter relief of coming clean. To admit to God that I am a sinner with no "But" attached runs so counterintuitive to us who have become experts at feigning innocence.

*Then Joshua said to Achan, 'My son, give glory to the Lord, the God of Israel, and honor him. Tell me what you have done; do not hide it from me.' Achan replied, 'It is true! I have sinned against the Lord, the God of Israel. This is what I have done.'*

**Joshua 7:19, 20 (NIV)**

We all want someone else to get us in shape. But at some point we realize that we are going to have to get our derriere to the gym. That means getting up in the morning, splashing water on our face, starting the car up in the freezing cold weather, driving to the gym, checking in, heading toward the locker room and…well, for some, this process alone is the workout.

And then there are those wonderful machines advertised on television as latest miracle. We didn't get this way overnight and we're not going to get in shape in a day no matter how much we want to believe the infomercials.

If our bodies can't be whipped into submission in one work-out, how much less can we expect this from our immortal souls?

And although we will have no reason to jog to the funeral parlor at our time of death, we will never outgrow our need for repentance and maintaining a right attitude toward God – even up to the last minute.

## PORTAL TO HEAVEN

We must keep our souls toned and in shape and that takes a determination on our part to remain brutally honest with God on a daily basis.

You'll get some pats on the back when you leave the gym.
You'll get the biggest embrace from God every time you repent.

*The LORD is near to all who call on him, to all who call on him in truth.*

**Psalm 145: 18 (NIV)**

One of the great tortures in life is not realizing our part in a conflict due to our own blindness or simply because the other party hurt us so terribly that all we could see were their faults.

This happened to me. Conviction of my role in a conflict had brought me to a dark place. I felt like Isaiah who, seeing his sin contrasted with the holiness of God, cries "Woe is me!"

In Isaiah's case, the Lord's angel touches his lips with coal and he is instantly clean.

In my case, I walked and did a double-take.

There seemed to be a rain that was exceptionally vivid and yet so imperceptible that it appeared not to be raining. I opened the screen door and there it was: a rain softer than a drizzle that would not chill me or soak me, but a rain so gentle with such soothing drops that it was like a sensitive massage from heaven.

## PORTAL TO HEAVEN

God was giving me a physical sign of the eternal reality of the softness of His forgiveness. Man is used to harsh and angry correction that can make it even harder for one to repent.

Yet Jesus, knowing how dark my sin would envelop me, had the forethought to literally touch me with a portal of cleansing rain that represented His reign of mercy over me.

*For God did not send his Son into the world to condemn the world, but to save the world through him.*

**John 3:17 (NIV)**

**Also Read: Isaiah 6:1-7 (NKJV) Isaiah 53:5 (KJV)**

# PEN YOUR PORTALS

The devil on one shoulder and the angel on the other is kid's stuff. But the cartoon characterization of the battle for our mind is not for adults.

There is a fight-to-the-finish over our minds and hearts. One key battle that feels like hand-to-hand combat is the one over our memories. Every day, our memories are either feeding our minds and hearts or they are sapping us and making us scared of the future.

The greatest sports competitors must win this battle immediately. The basketball guard who has the ball stolen at a critical time, the quarterback who threw a costly interception, the pitcher who threw a hanging curve late in the game and the coach who called a bad play all must *choose* to forget and look ahead or it will affect their *future* plays.

## PORTAL TO HEAVEN

Memories can trip us up in the present and cripple and destroy us in the long run. Approached rightly, they can also fill our minds with soul-satisfying instruction.

The best solution to controlling negative memories is filling our minds with scriptures that act as antidotes to these deadly cartoons. As these scriptures become imbedded in our souls, we will be able to win the battle over our memory and defeat the enemy like he is a... well, a cartoon character.

*Brothers, I do not consider myself yet to have laid hold of it. But one thing I do: Forgetting what is behind and straining toward what is ahead.*

**Philippians 3:13 (BSB)**

Can we really learn how to flip a memory for the positive?

This is a touchy area in some cases. For example, the death of a loved one might be hard to spin into a positive. Something heart-wrenching may need outside help from a trained source.

When I was in college, I got into the party scene and tried LSD. One such "trip" led me into thinking that all my roommates were against me when one accused me of not pulling my own weight. The paranoia destroyed my last semester and any hope of trusting anyone for a long time.

But what came out of it was that I indeed was "sponging." Fortunately, that memory got flipped and I was more aware of the need to pitch-in on many levels throughout my life.

On another occasion, a respected elderly person told me that I was pretentious. Because of the deep respect I had for this person, I was devastated for over a year. As I brought her almost flippant statement to God, I saw what this older person saw.

## PORTAL TO HEAVEN

God is a loving Father and it would be out of character for Him to burn memories into long-lasting regret without chance of redemption. Flipping a memory is like a reverse in wrestling. Let God help you flip the devil on the mat, pin him and win…and move on to the next match.

*He sent redemption unto his people…And the former things will not be remembered or come to mind.*

**Isaiah 65:17 (KJV), Psalm 111:9 (NAS)**

Why do we have memories in the first place?

There are obviously enough bad or tough ones to make some of us think that we'd be better off without detailed recollections.

If we could delete the unnecessary files in our brains like we do on the computer, we might have a faster "hard drive."

It isn't just the traumatic memories that seem to gunk up the processing within our brains. It's the little offenses and the unnecessary comments that can crash our hearts; even the petty hurts that happened a day or moments ago.

Obviously, God has given us memories so that we don't forget the tougher ones. These are called "lessons."

Some examples…I recall a bad financial investment. Ouch! I recall investments of time that left me looking at my watch. I'll never do that again! I recall investing in someone whom I knew in my gut would never be a good employee. Woe is me!

## PORTAL TO HEAVEN

The times we say "I'll never do that again" just happen to help us never do that again.

They also help others. We see someone about to step into the same trap that has been clawed into our memory and there are the rare birds that actually listen to us.

For all the others, they've been given this incredible thing called a memory.

*By the rivers of Babylon, There we sat down*
*and wept, when we remembered Zion.*

**Psalm 137:1 (NASB)**

Satan often likes to tweak memories in such a way so that we'll get them mixed up or so that he can use them to condemn us or to get us to conveniently revise and rearrange them so that we can escape repentance.

The beauty of Jesus was that He never let the guilty off the hook and yet He knew the perfect words to use with regard to the memory of their offense – all for the sake of bringing them to repentance.

What a contrast in style between Jesus and Satan!

In the case of a memory in which we own or share guilt, the other person might say, "You did this and caused that." If we were innocent, the devil might twist it to get us to believe we are guilty. Or Satan might remind us of how deeply we were wronged and therefore justified in renewing our anger.

Humility can help positively color memories. For those memories in which we were wronged, someone might put his arms around our shoulders and say, "Believe me, I understand what it means to forgive. Would you join me in this mission?" In the case of our guilt, that same friend might simply take the role of the most compassionate of confessors.

## PORTAL TO HEAVEN

When memories bring us closer to the God who resides where memories are only treasures, recollections can become rewritten history we know as redemption.

*Forget the former things; do not dwell on the past.*
*See, I am doing a new thing!*

**Isaiah 43:18,19 (NLT). Also Read: Philippians 3:13-14 (NIV)**

Instead of going for a planned walk, my brother took me for a stroll down Memory Lane via photos on his computer. It actually proved that our spiritual hearts needed more exercise than did our physical ones.

Neither of us is getting younger and aging has a way of playing games with recollections; specifically with regard to our life's worth and impact. Photos can be a good way of disciplining our memories.

In this case, the pictures brought to front and center images of our children. There were everyday snapshots, sports pictures, and graduation photos that reminded us that we had invested well. It was healthy for us to see how we spent our past.

## PORTAL TO HEAVEN

Minus a memory, our takes on our lives could be skewed one way or another and negatively colored by how things are going now. The danger there is that we could forget the good and impactful and that leads our steps toward remorse and regret. Whether through electronic or paper photos, a walk down Memory Lane has a way of clarifying the past no matter our season of life currently or how far geographically we are from where we first started life's walk.

*I remember You upon my bed and meditate on You in the night watches. For You have been my help, and in the shadow of Your wings will I rejoice… Remember the things I have done in the past. For I alone am God!…*

**Psalm 63:5-7 AMP, Isaiah 46:9,10 (NLT)**
**Also Read: Isaiah 43:18, Philippians 3:13-14**

# PEN YOUR PORTALS

"Dreams are what you have while you are sleeping; desires come while you are awake."

The Lord brought this word to me while watching The Oscars the year *La La Land* swept so many awards. The film is about the struggles two dreaming artists face in Los Angeles, or "City of Angels" as it is translated.

However, good angels don't get starry dreams mixed up with God-given desires when they deliver them to realm of humans. To be sure, God uses literal dreams as was the case for Old-Testament Joseph in Egypt and New-Testament Joseph in and out of Egypt.

What makes the dream/desire comparison more than semantics is that a dream can lead to a dead-end even if it is actually attained. On the other hand, a God-given dream will lead to the accomplishment of a heavenly directive and therefore its end will bear eternal fruit.

## PORTAL TO HEAVEN

*La La Land* represents the world's reality and what it honors. While *La La Land* was well done, its title is fitting for the mindset of members of The Academy who selected Moonlight for Best Film over Hacksaw Ridge – a true story about a World War II hero who only his faith could dream up.

*Delight yourself in the LORD, and he will give you the desires of your heart… trust in the Lord with all your heart; do not depend on your own understanding. Seek his will in all you do, and he will show you which path to take.*

**Psalm 37:4 (ESV), Proverbs 3:5,6 (NLT)**
**Also read: Matthew 6:33 (ESV)**

"God gave us His life so we could give our life to Him to attain that same life."

This was the word that God gave as I read, "The lamp of the body is the eye. If therefore your eye is good, your whole body will be full of light."

Who wouldn't we want to walk around shining all the time?

Yet, there is part of us that either does not let God in completely so that the "whole body is full of light" or that He could pull off such a trick with little ole us.

Either way, this is sin; straightforward sin.

But God promised this life of shining for everyone regardless of their station in life or education. This has phenomenal implications. This life is accessible. It's simple. He always intended it to be so.

And this includes us.

## PORTAL TO HEAVEN

God's presence is very accessible through moment-by-moment portals in which we see heaven through things on earth. Through our senses, He is indeed within us through His Holy Spirit working to make our "whole body" full of light so that we become the shining people we were intended to be because of this life-for-life exchange.

Oh God, help our unbelief.

*This is how God showed his love among us: He sent his one and only Son into the world that we might live through him.*

**1 John 4:9 (NIV)**

**Also read: Psalm 27:4 (HCSB), Mark 9:24 (NIV)**

A friend has a modest pick-up truck that he has had so long that he had to overhaul it. Though not the truck love affair that some have, it certainly could be termed an "affection."

I always admired him because a truck is a favor-magnet. Someone would walk up to him at church and he knew just where the conversation was headed.

"Hey Dave, "I have this refrigerator…"

"Hey Dave, "I don't suppose you have any free time Saturday morning?"

He would never act annoyed. In fact, I came to realize that it blessed him to help all of these people. Beyond the truck, he lent himself as well. Dave's physical labor became part of the package.

I don't know whether his desire to own a truck and all that it represented included a foreknowledge of what a favor-magnet it would turn out to be.

## PORTAL TO HEAVEN

The truck is a symbol of the cross. It carried people and their "baggage" from one place to another. His giving of himself was like that of Jesus in that he'd put everything into moving that fridge or piece of furniture. Desires are a funny thing. They might start out innocent enough. But when completely given over to God, they are the vehicles that transport us on the road to Calvary.

*…the Son of Man did not come to be served, but to serve, and to give his life as a ransom for many…[Jesus] emptied Himself, taking the form of a bond-servant.*

**Matthew 20:28 (NIV), Philippians 2:7 (NASB)**

"Marriage is a great institution…if you like institutions."

If you're single and in your twenties, that's a great line. But after you fall in love, you don't see its humor – just the desires of romance, sex and companionship.

Jesus said that "from the beginning," marriage was to be two souls becoming one and that divorce was for the hard-hearted.

It was as if He was saying that the hardness of marriage is where the divine mysteries lay. That's heaven's counter-punch line to the aforementioned one-liner. The reason why marriage is so difficult is that the differences between women and men are designed to bring sacrifice out of ourselves.

## PORTAL TO HEAVEN

The natural desires for intimacy that draw us into relationships are the very desires of God. Through this union, we get one of the clearest portals into heaven's Holy Trinity. In other words, He knew this when He designed all of the wonders of romance.

Whether you think romance and marriage is God's way of tricking us into a sacrificial life or whether you're actually enjoying the ride or if you're still in the pre-marriage arena, you've probably figured out by now that you can get to like the institutions of God.

*As written in Scripture, 'The two become one.' Since we want to become spiritually one with the Master, we must not pursue the kind of sex that avoids commitment and intimacy, leaving us lonelier than ever—the kind of sex that can never 'become one.'…*

**Galatians 6:16, 17 (The Message)**
**Also read: Matthew 19:8 (NIV) & (NLT), Ecclesiastes 4:10 (NIV)**

As a writer, I love to watch movie credits. The credits take so long to sit through and yet that is where the work of the movie is exposed.

If marriage were a movie, the credits might be something that is read by astute children and grandchildren. The movie itself might have some good-looking actors, subplots, special effects and an even a moving story line.

But that's just what you see on the screen… a relationship where the conception may have been eyes that met, an admiration of a quality or talent or some other attraction that sets two souls toward marriage.

If romantic desire were a staircase, it surely leads up to a family. One desire builds upon the next. Before long, there's a grandchild in the bassinet.

Looking back to my youth, a grandchild was only something we spoke about in terms of, "That'll be something to tell your grandkids."

## PORTAL TO HEAVEN

The unsuspecting youngster who desires a lover has no idea just how long those credits will ultimately take to role. When marriages are permitted to be made in heaven, all of the credit will go to a very patient, longsuffering God.

*Then Esau looked up and saw the women and children. 'Who are these with you?' he asked. Jacob answered, 'They are the children God has graciously given your servant.'*

**Genesis 33:5 (NIV)**
**Also read: 1 Samuel 1:27, 28 (NIV), Hebrews 12:2a (KJV)**

I pay attention to my projections and hopes for the New Year because they are often a microcosm of my life.

One of the all-time leaders on the typical New Year's resolutions chart is that of getting in shape and losing weight. We all know that a mere 6-9 miles of walking each week could make a huge impact on our health.

So, I resolutely decided to put faith into action by going out for a morning walk. My property has flatlands and hills. By the grace of God, He took me by the hand to the level ground first…and with good reason. A recurring hip-flexor strain likes to visit me.

If I had begun to exercise on the hills, my hip flexor would have reminded me that it is walking right alongside me. But if I start on the flatlands, I can warm up and stretch a little before I get to the hills and mitigate the stress on my hip. I can't afford to pull a muscle because it would also impact all of the other goals on my New Year's list.

## PORTAL TO HEAVEN

God-inspired New Year's Resolutions lead to winnable tasks. Small victories lead to bigger ones. By listening to Him, I am in the warm-up period of my New Year and "hip" to the temptation to walk ahead of The Lord.

*Do not despise these small beginnings, for the Lord rejoices to see the work begin…*

**Zechariah 4:10 (NLT)**

I once attended a ribbon-cutting ceremony of a trailhead created to encircle a golf course. It was part of the green movement utilizing wooded areas within communities and around open spaces in an effort to get people exercising while familiarizing them with the outdoors right under their noses.

Whether it's a path around a golf course or the border of houses in the suburbs or a rail trail along a river, these paths allow users to see nature up close and from a perspective that would otherwise remain unseen.

While salvation is not through even the holiest of former or contemporary saints, it is wise for us to see the paths they have pioneered. And while we're walking or biking, we may even feel the bond of such paths knowing that others have been down this road. It's a great way to "join" them, as it were.

## PORTAL TO HEAVEN

Godly pioneers of the past have cleared some distinct paths from their life experience with Jesus. Today, there are probably a few trailblazers in our lives. It's good to notice when they are having a ribbon-cutting and humbly bring a pair of scissors to both recognize their work and get a good start on that path.

*Do you see what this means—all these pioneers who blazed the way, all these veterans cheering us on? It means we'd better get on with it. Strip down, start running—and never quit! ... Keep your eyes on Jesus, who both began and finished this race we're in.*

**Hebrews 12:1, 2 (The Message)**

Some feel that trees look too barren without leaves. However, there are advantages to "seeing the forest through the trees."

I found myself scouting out my property to discover potential paths for walking, biking, and other activities. Alongside this aspiration is my desire to construct wooden meditation benches at certain scenic or contemplative spots – especially next to places with water.

The lack of leaves allowed me to see prospective paths; a great use of the seemingly "barren" times. Some of these paths have great potential and yet are strewn with fallen trees right across them.

## PORTAL TO HEAVEN

God does the same thing with our lives. We see forests. He sees paths. He goes before us and blazes trails. Some will be a walk in the park, designed for leisure and smooth sailing. Some will be steep inclines where we re-tie our shoes so as not to hurt ourselves. There are also deeper and darker valley paths where the sun can't seem to reach. Other trails are designed next to bubbling streams or larger bodies of water. Certain ones will steer us to a pond-side bench, the equivalent to "leading me beside still waters."

Look in a new light at the fallen trees that stubbornly block some of our potential paths. Perhaps it's time to use these roadblocks for benches.

*He refreshes my soul [especially at the New Year], He guides me along the right paths for his name's sake.*

**Psalm 23:3 (NIV) [Brackets not from King David]**

Planning for the year ahead can make us feel as vulnerable as the sheep in Psalm 23. These lambs really don't know where they are going. They are simply led. So, it's one step at a time following a voice command, and occasionally, a gentle or swift poke in the butt.

In a word, they trust. That is what I noticed one time in Jerusalem where sheep were barely inching their way along a trail. As the shepherd got to some rather large bushes, the sheep seemed to disappear into them. It must have been thirty minutes before he got them out of there, rounded them back up and continued on his journey.

## PORTAL TO HEAVEN

Sheep don't think ahead. They are led. Whether it's feeding, rest, protection, direction or whatever, they simply rely on their leader.

In terms of trusting God's vision for our lives, those who claim to follow The Good Shepherd could learn a lot from dumb sheep as we plan our year ahead, make intricate goals and envision dreams that we consider so dear to us.

*He leads me…*

**Psalm 23:2b (ESV)**
**Also read: Psalm 23 in entirety**

"...the future starts now! God is keeping careful watch over us and the future. The Day is coming when you'll have it all—life healed and whole."*

Is it this a televangelist, a positive-thinker or a member of the Optimist Club? Actually, St. Peter would be the correct answer.

He continues:
"I know how great this makes you feel, even though you have to put up with every kind of aggravation in the meantime. Pure gold put in the fire comes out of it *proved* pure; genuine faith put through this suffering comes out *proved* genuine. When Jesus wraps this all up, it's your faith not your gold, that God will have on display as evidence of his victory." (1 Peter 1:6,7)

## ᏢORTAL ᏟᎢO ᎻEAVEN

If you are one who dangles on the verge of optimism and pessimism simultaneously and can't figure out why you suffer from a bit of vertigo, think no more. Juxtaposition is one of those ways that God shows our need for Him. It's also a reality check. Life is not usually an either-or.

We could look ahead to the year ahead and grapple to make it fit into a tamed narrative. But when we get to Heaven's Gate, Pete may be swapping some stories and chuckles about New Year's Resolutions.

*Your life is a journey you must travel with a deep consciousness of God ... It's because of this sacrificed Messiah ... that you trust God, that you know you have a future in God.*

**1 Peter 1:18,21(The Message)**
**\* 1 Peter 1:4,5 (The Message)**

# PEN YOUR PORTALS

# February

## PORTALS TO HEAVEN

There once was a year of comebacks.
In basketball, the Cleveland Cavaliers mustered a NBA
Championship from a 3 games-to-1 deficit.
In baseball, the Cleveland Indians let go of a 3-1 lead over the
Chicago Cubs in the World Series.
In football, the New England Patriots overcame a 28-3 lead by The
Atlanta Falcons to win the Super Bowl.

But the biggest upset didn't happen in sports. The political theater
ushered in a historic win with the election of Donald Trump. He
was behind in many polls, made a lot of enemies, and didn't have
the backing of his own party in many cases. He had no political
experience and he was running against one of the biggest names
in modern-day politics.

What is the cosmic-comeback message here?

## PORTAL TO HEAVEN

Whether our team or candidate was on the right side of the victory,
we all need to witness comebacks because at some point – perhaps
now or soon – we will be in need of one. There is no way out of it.
There is a way through it.

The end of the comeback may not leave us in a glorious spotlight
holding onto a coveted trophy, but it will certainly leave us holding
the hand of Christ who upholds us in all things.

*For though I fall, I will rise again. Though I sit in darkness, the LORD will
be my light… in him [Christ] all things hold together…*

**Micah 7:8 (NLT), Colossians 1:17 (ESV), Editor's brackets.**
**Also read: Hebrews 1:3 (NASB), Proverbs 24:16 (NLT)**

It's easy to look at roadblocks, setbacks and outright failures as impediments to our goals.

Whether its family issues, job challenges or financial difficulties, it's tempting to fall into discouragement over our situations.

When I was younger, my finances were like the drought that revealed the stones at the bottom of the reservoir. I truly understood the term, "rock bottom."

That desperation led me to be in a position to take a job that I never would have entertained. I received a phone call inviting me to work for a senior citizen organization. That one job led to a life-changing career.

In this case, some humbling failures led me to see that the job was heaven-sent. He really does give us "beauty for ashes."

## PORTAL TO HEAVEN

Opportunities may be orchestrated by God - even when they come with a little camouflage.

*Goliath stood and shouted to the ranks of Israel... 'Choose a man and have him come down to me. If he is able to fight and kill me, we will become your subjects; but if I overcome him and kill him, you will become our subjects and serve us'... David said to [Goliath], 'You come against me with sword and spear and javelin, but I come against you in the name of the Lord Almighty'... Reaching into his bag and taking out a stone, he slung it and struck the Philistine on the forehead. The stone sank into his forehead, and he fell facedown on the ground.*

**1 Samuel 17:8,45,49 (NIV)**

Throughout scripture, disguised-opportunity stories abound. But there is one where it looks as if all hope is lost.

A man destined to be king named David was chased out of his land by his jealous father-in-law-king.

It gets worse. It's so bad that David goes to work for the enemy of his king. Immediately before David is to go fight against his father-in-law and his best friend, his new king fears that he'll switch devotion back to his old country and so orders David to leave.

It gets worse. David returns to the town where the wives and children of he and his men were staying only to find them taken away by raiders.

It gets worse. The men somehow blame David and some talk of stoning him.

It gets better. David went on to raid those who had kidnapped the families and obtained so much plunder that he had enough left over to share with the elders of his former country which helped paved the way for his return.

Moreover, the battle that he was not allowed to fight was the very one where his king and best friend were killed and this vacancy led to David's ascension to the throne.

## ᑭORTAL ᑤO ᒍHEAVEN

Life is stranger than fiction. When it comes with a little drama, it doesn't mean that God isn't writing it.

*But David strengthened himself in the Lord his God.*

**1 Samuel 30:6 (ESV)**

**Also read: 1 Samuel 17**

When I was young in my faith, I fixated on my sins. For some, this is a natural thing to do. For others, they couldn't understand why I couldn't figure out that I was forgiven.

The issue was very simple: Since my sin was prevalent every day, I couldn't see The Savior through my sin.

My wise pastor instructed me to reverse my mindset and focus on The Savior instead of the sin. From there on in, I did better.

Sin is like that. Mistakes are like that. We can choose to focus on our failures or we can be students of grace - which incidentally humbles.

In my case, I wished that I had read C.S. Lewis' great "peace" of advice from *Mere Christianity*: "On the whole, God's love for us is a much safer subject to think about than our love for Him."*

## ᏢORTAL ᏟTO ᎻEAVEN

Sins and concurring mistakes are the golden grace-pavers on the road to eternity. Could this be why heaven's streets are made of gold?

*But [The Lord] said to me, 'My grace is sufficient for you, for my power is made perfect in weakness.' Therefore I will boast all the more gladly about my weaknesses, so that Christ's power may rest on me… What then shall we say? Shall we continue in sin so that grace may increase? By no means!*

**2 Corinthians 12:9 (NIV), Romans 6:1 (BSB)**

**Editor's brackets**

*Mere Christianity*, by C.S. Lewis, Chapter Nine

When the sun rises, it's the birth of a new day with new opportunities.

When I walk through the door of my office, I am not only greeted by people, but with opportunity.

The most dangerous moments have come when my day or moment became so mundane that I didn't serve or smile or think as I ought.

It wasn't a missed opportunity because I lost an advantage financially or in some other way. I blew an assignment. Someone got hurt and it's not just the hurt of the one we didn't serve properly.

It's God himself. It's like the dad who notices on a beautiful spring day that the cherished bike he bought for his son is lying in the garage because the video game in the dark bedroom upstairs seemed easier.

As sure as that scrambling squirrel or that singing cardinal in our yards have a peppy place in our day, there's a specific role within our day. It may be as simple as unscrewing a jar lid that was too hard for my wife. That's still an opportunity given by God himself.

## PORTAL TO HEAVEN

Opportunity doesn't "just knock once" as the old saying goes. It's ever before us once we understand the context of why we were given life and how it can affect so many. We could look ahead to the year ahead and grapple to make it fit into a tamed narrative. But when we get to Heaven's Gate, Pete may be swapping some stories and chuckles about New Year's Resolutions.

*Make the most of every opportunity in these evil days...Be wise in the way you act toward outsiders; make the most of every opportunity.*

**Ephesians 5:16 (NLT), Colossians 4:5 (NIV)**

I am not a voracious hunter of Christian legends, saints and holidays when there are debatable facts surrounding such history.

Valentine is no exception in my book. Some may pierce his heart with an arrow aimed at faulty folklore. I would rather hand the bow to cupid and let him take aim at our motives.

As in Valentine's day, paganism remains rampant today. It's understandable that sincere Christians are concerned about the origins of holidays. But now, the pendulum has swung toward debunking Christian saints and tossing them on the garbage dump of urban legend and crediting secularism for their holidays.

It's possible that Valentine handed a letter on the day of his execution to the girl he healed of blindness and signed it, "Your Valentine." Whether true or not, there is a real possibility that he was stoned, clubbed and beheaded for his unflinching faith in Jesus.

## ᏢORTAL ᏟO ᕼEAVEN

Valentine encourages me to use symbols of Christ that I see every day and everywhere. Cupid is too big for my tub, but I'm not going to throw out the baby Jesus with the bathwater. In fact, we should start naming babies "Valentine" and let them grow up explaining why.

*And no wonder, for Satan himself masquerades as an angel of light…*

**2 Corinthians 11:14 (NIV)**

The month of February is a great time to probe deeper into flowers and chocolate because we may find they have a sweeter meaning than meets the eye and tastebuds.

God brings "lovers" like Valentine into our life to teach us how to love. Why would the holiday that represents the heart be celebrated during the dead of winter?

Valentine was a great bishop who lived when the "dead" of winter was year-round. That is, Christians were being martyred then through much of the Roman Empire.

Supposedly, his crime was centered on his passion for Christ. He converted Roman citizens and that brought them away from the idolatry of worshipping their Roman emperors as gods. He also married young couples and that impinged on the recruitment of young men for military service. Valentine paid for his "treason" with his blood and perhaps that's the reason that the color red is associated with him. Throughout history, anonymous courageous men and women put their lives on the line "for God and country" and this is why those like Valentine touch our heartstrings in February and all year around.

## PORTAL TO HEAVEN

Valentine's life helps us see the pattern that God employs during the darkest of times when everything seems blacker than dark chocolates and colder than February 14th. After all, Jesus wasn't sent at Israel's high point.

*For if they do these things when the wood is green, what will happen when it is dry?*

**1 Samuel 17:8,45,49 (NIV)**

Valentine's Month wouldn't be complete without a word about lips and kisses.

We start life bathed in kisses. We don't remember being smothered in love, but we were. After that, we learn to give kisses away. We're even encouraged to kiss that great-great aunt that we've never seen before. It makes us feel uncomfortable, but it makes her day; maybe her year.

Then, there are those smooches at bedtime. "Kisses, and all that" was our favorite expression when tucking our kids into bed. We'd watch them curl up and eventually witness those eyes giving way to the secure dreams those kisses helped induce.

Kisses may get a little too sugary around Valentine's Day with those little heart-shaped candies and chocolates. But, we love those homemade cards.

If we're not careful around puberty, kisses can be fairly exciting, unfortunately too common, and more than a bit premature. But kisses given to the one we wed can be so erotic, fulfilling and magical that we wake up and wonder if it was all a dream. Psychologists have found that sex can outlast kissing as couples age. Evidently, kisses are intimacy's secret.

## PORTAL TO HEAVEN

Kissing is a metaphor that points straight to intimacy with God. If I could remember what it was like to be bathed in kisses as a baby, how might I then daily use these lips?

*Set a guard, O LORD, over my mouth; Keep watch over the door of my lips…*

**Psalm 141:3 (NIV)**

**Also read: Song of Solomon 5:16, James 3:9-11**

Theologians aside, it is my shoot-from-the-hip theory that we can learn a lot from the way we celebrate Valentine's Day.

Candy and roses represent the sweet side of love. Hey, nothing wrong with that. Every time a child kisses me on the cheek, I am forever indebted to the sweetness of love.

The manner in which we celebrate Valentine's Day is representative of the way we view love. It's all wine and roses.

But what happens when love ain't so sweet? What happens when love's kitchen turns up the heat under a soup made of mortgage payments, deadlines, four cavities and the dog just pooped on the living room rug? When love is literally and figuratively exhausted, what's next? That's where love begins.

A father-in-the-faith once told me that when your love is pointed toward the other person and their needs are above our own, that's true love. Perhaps that's too long of an explanation to fit on one of those disgusting-tasting miniature hearts.

Our culture sells the kind of love that sells. Who buys that but those that truly believe that sweetness equates to it tasting good for me – like chocolate on Valentine's Day.

## PORTAL TO HEAVEN

The kingdom of heaven is an inverted one that is sweetest when it is serving. At the risk of ruining anyone's image of Valentine's Day, this includes cleaning up that which resembles melted chocolate on the rug.

*Greater love has no one than this: to lay down one's life for one's friends.*

**1 Samuel 17:8,45,49 (NIV)**

Ah, the bitter-sweetness of love...
*Lo, who canst reveal, the hard ground to cover*
*To the soft-soil center of the new blind lover?*
*The thorn on the rose, from head to toes*
*Deceives so well, thy eyes and nose.* *

Have you ever wondered why roses are the symbolic favorite for Valentine's Day and for love on a host of other occasions? Is it really justifiable to assign this species to love when such delicate pedals are supported by an executioner of the fingertips?

Any lover who's been around the block could answer that. Even most teens can ouch-out that true or false question. The moment you fall in or allow for love is the very second that you put yourself in a position to be pricked instead of picked.

Roses conjure up images of smitten love or wildly romantic stories. Indeed, there is that side. One visit to The International Rose Test Garden in Portland could get you fixated on innocence of the flower. You'd be stunned by the subtle and radical differences of the scents. And the colors and 550 varieties add to the overload of the sweetness of this "singular" species. But even on the most dedicated and skilled gardener's glove lie bloodstains from this labor of love.

## ᑭORTAL ᑕTO ᕼEAVEN

It comes in question form: "If love never hurts, is it really love at all?" How blessed am I that as I embrace Christ's body, my hands are smeared with the blood of Christ without enduring the thorns that only He could bear.

*I am the Rose of Sharon...an aroma from life to life...a sweet aroma from life to life...*

**Song of Solomon 2:1(KJV), 2 Corinthians 14:16 (NASB)**
**\* *The Rose* by Robert J. LaCosta**

# PEN YOUR PORTALS

A lot was at stake. Mom's 80th birthday was around the corner. She had just come through a serious operation with a longer-than-expected recovery and we wanted to celebrate her life and her courage. She had said she'd like to go on a picnic. It seemed a bit understated for such a milestone. But Mom's preference matched her childlike heart.

We chose a little resort town that she loved in The Adirondack Mountains – notorious for sudden and dangerous thunderstorms. We were pinned down to one date due to family schedules. From there, it was a week of checking the weather app.

Being "reduced" to prayer sounds like an oxymoron. Yet, that is what outdoor events do to you. The weather report was not looking good. When the day arrived for the picnic, I checked my phone one more time and rain was now predicted from noon through 2 p.m. – the exact time of our picnic.

I was reduced to prayer. "Lord, if it must, let it rain all around us except where we are having the picnic." Now, I was the childlike one having nothing else to do but depend on Father God. It rained over the lake to the north and the mountains to the south while our childlike matriarch enjoyed a picnic under blue skies.

## PORTAL TO HEAVEN

I might not have prayed about the weather had it looked more favorable. That's a lot like life. We believe it's on some sort of autopilot until we are forced to look up at clouds…and beyond.

*Is anyone among you in trouble? Let them pray…never stop praying.*

**James 5:13 (NIV), 1 Thessalonians 5:17 (NLT)**

We have all wrestled with prayer and cancer. Someone we dearly love had been diagnosed with this advanced-stage killer and this led to thinking about the Hezekiah-healing prayer.*

The prophet Isaiah told the gravely-ill King Hezekiah, "Put your house in order, because you are going to die; you will not recover." With bitter tears, Hezekiah reminded God of his faithfulness. God then told Isaiah to return and deliver a new message: "I have heard your prayer and seen your tears; I will heal you...I will add fifteen years to your life. And I will deliver you and this city..."

If only all cancer stories ended that way. When the sudden and fatal diagnosis came regarding my mother's colon cancer, I prayed for weeks for her healing. A few months later, I prayed that the Lord would take her. Was one prayer better than the other?

A faith-filled prayer and one of presumption can be separated by the thinnest of lines. We must lean heavily on what we think The Holy Spirit within us is saying. We hope for confirmation from mature believers.

But leaning on experience alone is danger. If a prayer seemed to be answered "favorably" one time, it doesn't mean the same will be repeated...and vice versa.

## PORTAL TO HEAVEN

The Holy Spirit must be given such reign for this and other reasons in our lives so we don't wrestle as much with reason and logic, but whether we are allowing Him to lead us away from presumption and into the throne room of God.

*...the Spirit himself intercedes for us through wordless groans.*

**Romans 8:26 (NIV); *The Hezekiah Healing: See 2 Kings 20**

You're walking in a familiar and lovely spot when a squirrel runs by and darts up a tree as if he thinks your Daniel Boone. An immediate thought about running away from relationships comes to mind and within a second, you find yourself talking about it with the one you're with.

You're looking over a scenic area and it takes your breadth away. You pause. You have to take it in even though you may not be the stop-and-smell-the-roses type. You shake your head and sigh and your friend does the same.

You hang up the phone and feel a surging stirring for the person you were speaking with and what they are going through. You immediately sit down at the dining room table and share their sad story with your friend.

These unplanned talks are becoming more frequent. They offer an outlet where you are free to speak plainly. You feel completely understood. You begin to wonder, "Am I getting more out of his listening or his responses?" You settle on both. Why set up a false dichotomy?

You bump into someone at the grocery story that you haven't seen for a while. Their cart is loaded down and so is their heart. You say, "I'd like to introduce you to my friend."

## PORTAL TO HEAVEN

Pray constantly… [Jesus] comforts us in all our troubles, so that we can comfort those in any trouble with the comfort we ourselves receive from God…By day the Lord directs his love, at night his song is with me – a prayer to the God of my life.

*And no wonder, for Satan himself masquerades as an angel of light…*

**1 Thessalonians 5:17 (HCSB), 2 Corinthians 1:4 (NIV)**
**[Editor's brackets], Psalm 42:8 (NIV)**

Whether it's a figurative or literal stretch (think yawning during devotions), praise and thanksgiving can be prayer.

It has been said, "He who sings prays twice."

It's hard not to thank God for food. It's hard not to marvel at the top of our game or the top of a mountain.

When we speak with a friend, child, spouse or whoever and we compliment them on their character or their completion of this or that or we praise their nature of giving or for some incredible selfless act, are we not still talking with them?

It's the same with God.

We may have been taught that prayer is petition. Even "The Lord's Prayer" could be viewed in such a fashion. We may have been taught to "seek His face and not His hand."

It might have been hammered into our consciousness that we are to memorize prayers or format them in a certain way.

These may all be well and good. But if my young or adult child comes up to me and praises and thanks me for a benevolent act or my faithfulness to them, I'd consider that a "conversation" of the highest quality.

## PORTAL TO HEAVEN

Praise and thanks is a good way to start off any chat. It may even develop into a deep conversation.

*Enter his gates with thanksgiving and his courts with praise; give thanks to him and praise his name.*

**Psalm 100:4 (NIV)**

Just what is so endearing about individually or corporately praying *The Lord's Prayer*? And how about when it's sung and chills run down your spine?

Is it the universality of its strains? Could it be that it was Jesus' personal prayer to his Father – a secret code, if you will? Is it because it addresses just about every concern the way a multi-vitamin covers all the bases?

Whether overtly or subtly, the *Our Father* puts us in our place. You and I immediately take our position as those conceived by one who came before us. That is quite extraordinary considering many of us may subconsciously think we are tackling this thing called "life" all by ourselves. It is not true.

We were put here and like all good families, we have our place and mission. We are to make His kingdom come. It's as if He is handing us a laminated brochure of heaven and sending us on our way to both explain and sell the ultimate retirement locale. The rest of the prayer borrows on the logistics of accomplishing this purpose…food for the body and a bath for the soul.

But there is more than sheer understanding that Jesus was getting across to us.

## PORTAL TO HEAVEN

At its heart, *The Lord's Prayer* is a window into the relationship that Jesus has with his Father. When prayer becomes relationship, we understand the appeal and the peace of *Our Father*.

*The Father and I are one… For this reason I bow my knees to the Father of our Lord Jesus Christ, from whom the whole family in heaven and earth is named…*

**John 10:30 (HCSB), Ephesians 3:14 (NKJV)**

# PEN YOUR PORTALS

My staff used to chuckle when they'd witness me holding a different phone in each ear and my mobile on speaker. I'd run into one exam room, then into the next to see if the issue was a quick fix, then get back to the patient in the first exam room before welcoming some in the waiting room before another round of... you guessed it, phone calls.

When the buy-out for that practice transpired, I found myself busy with my new career in writing. However, I haven't since simultaneously fielded three phone calls nor have I heard any of the ups and downs of the elderly in the exam rooms. Instead, this writer's computer screen seemed to ask me, "Is anyone out there?"

It was after I opened up a small hearing aid practice a few years later that I realized the origin of some of my loneliness. I had inadvertently isolated myself from The River of Suffering. Getting back into serving the elderly was one of the best remedies for my ironic "affliction." After all, I knew better than anyone that hearing loss isolates its victims.

As strange as it will sound to those looking forward to retirement or a way out of their current job, situation or discomfort of any kind, I have some advice that as a writer I am obliged to share: never try to get away consciously or subconsciously from The River of Suffering.

## PORTAL TO HEAVEN

More than anybody, Jesus knows what He is doing when He throws us back into The River of Suffering – sink or swim.

*Carry each other's burdens, and in this way you will fulfill the law of Christ.*

**Galatians 6:2 (NIV)**

Mothers tend to have a special place in our hearts because they carried us within themselves. You can't get much closer to someone's heart. They suffer through countless illnesses and discomforts that they alone know. It's no wonder they are with us through thick and thin.

Shared suffering connects souls. This is why battalions have reunions fifty years later and why leaders are revered by their followers. It's the inspiration of statues and why streets and cities are named after them.

While many of us nudge up to the edge of The River of Suffering in our own lives, others are rowing vigorously within it. Others have been thrown out and are crying for life preservers.

This may seem extreme and far removed from our civilized culture. But the concept of suffering "tying us" to other souls is not. We can or should be able to relate to those we have suffered for and with and the effect that has on our prayer life.

I may never know the extent of suffering that some are experiencing. Disease, illness, Third-World pain and the like may not have overflowed the banks of my River of Suffering.

## PORTAL TO HEAVEN

Suffering has a force that is unlike any other when it comes to birthing prayer and empathy. It puts a deeper spin on the reality of there being a blessing on the tie that binds.

*…You keep track of all my sorrows. You have collected all my tears in your bottle. You have recorded each one in your book.*

**Psalm 56:8 (NLT)**
**Also read: Philippians 3:10, Acts 9:16, & The Nicene Creed**

The *Insanity of God* is a documentary that begins with a missionary couple that suffers through the brokenness of the nation of Somalia while losing their teenage son.

Propelled by a spiritual instinct to search deeper for God and the secrets of the tenacity of persecuted Christians around the world, Nik and Ruth Ripken found themselves in dozens of countries where Nik privately interviewed many believers who have suffered through the unimaginable.

After scores of these clandestine encounters, the missionaries began to uncover a "common courage" that most of us have never experienced.

In one segment, a man filled with bitterness over an invading country's presence cannot seem to wash the blood off his hands from killing over 150 of those invaders. After finding Christ, he is cleansed and begins to smuggle bibles. He even lets go of the one thing he is holding back from God: his wife and children. He eventually includes them in his ministry, concluding that Jesus would be worth the unthinkable if it ever came to that.

This documentary reveals the correlation between suffering and the will of God, or as the film calls it, the "insanity" of God. Those forced to live daily with such "common courage" have discovered that same "insanity;" this heart of Jesus.

## PORTAL TO HEAVEN

The more we suffer for Christ, the more we understand His suffering for us. We have something "in common" with The Creator.

*God is not ashamed to be called their God, for he has prepared a city for them.*

**Read: Hebrews 11:16 (NIV)**

"Sticks and stones may break my bones but names will never hurt me."

While that nursery-rhyme-type adage is about name-calling, it has a broader implication with respect to emotional pain. Those who suffer like this will tell you that their suffering is as real as any physical problem.

The only solace I can offer those who occasionally or chronically ache from mental or emotional illness is that it is possible to receive help from God. If such suffering is self-inflicted, it can be helped and/or cured through repentance as it says in Psalm 34:18b: "[God] saves such as have a contrite spirit." (NKJV)

If the ache comes from the blows of life, they can be relieved from the reassurance that God is near: "If your heart is broken, you'll find God right there…" (Psalm 34:18a, The Message)

There are countless ways that the heart can be broken. Unfortunately, it affects our every breadth and even invades our dreams. Emotional weight may seem as heavy as any physical pain we've ever lifted.

## PORTAL TO HEAVEN

The sticks and stones of emotional pain may not be able to be dodged, but there is one name that will never hurt you.

*God keeps an eye on his friends, his ears pick up every moan and groan…Is anyone crying for help? God is listening, ready to rescue you.*

**Psalm 34: 15,17 (The Message)**

It was a morning like any other morning. Got up. Sipped some water. Fed the cats. Made sure Katy had her bowl safely distanced from Mercy's food. Katy likes her space.

I wondered if she had been on the trail of the baby mouse that casually sauntered out to nibble on a piece of cat food that had dropped off the side of the kitty dish. I purposely placed the cat bowl near where the mouse appeared to see if Katy-The-Master-Hunter would pick up the scent. And yet, Katy appeared uninterested.

After feeding them, I walked to the back door only to see the remains of the poor little mouse. Katy had just vomited the creature in our hallway and here I thought she was just being fussy. I had misjudged her. On the outside, she looked like the same cat.

## PORTAL TO HEAVEN

I can misjudge that someone is fine because they look good or normal on the outside when they are actually having a rough day, week, year or…life. And sometimes, though we are ignorant of their situation or not as perceptive as we ought to be, our role may be to let them throw up and clean up the mess.

*Seeing the people, [Jesus] felt compassion for them, because they were distressed and dispirited like sheep without a shepherd.*

**Matthew 9:36 (KJV). Editor's Brackets.**

# PEN YOUR PORTALS

# March

## PORTALS TO HEAVEN

"March Madness" is a phrase often associated with the NCAA College Basketball tournament that turns sports bars and couches into places of crazy emotion. But March Madness could also be the result of cabin fever for us northerners.

You expect near-zero wind-chill in January. But when it makes you tighten your scarf and look down for self-protection, you know it's March. It makes for madness.

It's like this. The March crocus that peeps up in your garden symbolizes all of the goose bumps of promise for another year of spring flowers, dreams of opening the swimming pool, long days, a chance to peel off layers, the return of the hummingbirds and all of the green, green grass of home.

And so much more.

For many, the warmer weather represents the softer side of Mother Nature and life. Motorcycles come out. Bikes join them. Tops go down on convertibles. Dog leashes are heard outside your screen window. Ice cream stands open. Even rain feels kinder and gentler. Oh, happy day.

And then you wake up the next day and look out the window and snow is falling on your precious crocus.

## PORTAL TO HEAVEN

March symbolizes a lot of dreams that get put off…and some indefinitely. Even if it feels that God can't be seen in March, He sure can be heard. These early birds seem louder in March as if they were sent by God to tell those northern weather fronts of discouragement, "I'll show you." Crazy, huh?

*Hope deferred makes the heart sick, but a longing fulfilled is a tree of life…*
*He who testifies to these things says, 'Yes, I am coming soon.' Amen. Come,*
*Lord Jesus.*

**Proverbs 13:12 (NIV), Revelation 22:20 (NIV)**

The unpredictability of life...

I grew up in New Jersey where the saying went, "If you don't like the weather here, stick around for a minute." Sure, we had the reliable four seasons. Generally, flowers would begin budding in April...unless you get that April 6th snowstorm. But then again, just wait a minute.

One March day, upstate New York took a page out of Jersey's game book. Weather went from the sixties in late February to zero-wind chill in just under sixty seconds, or so it seemed. On top of that, three feet of snow was literally on top of that.

Anyone for a quick trip to Disney? Oh, wait a minute. The flights are all cancelled. Well, maybe some shopping at the mall? Oh, boy, their employees can't make it in. Just go get some groceries? Oh my, the shelves are nearly empty.

There is a deep desire within every person to control his or her life as if they would be their own god.

## PORTAL TO HEAVEN

The unpredictability of weather is one of the clearest daily reminders that God is in charge. We are not in control of half of what we think we are. But God uses the "wait-a-minute" of Mother Nature to get people shifting from talking about the weather to talking about Him – whether in a state of panic or in the State of New Jersey.

*He said to them, 'Why are you afraid, you men of little faith?' Then He got up and rebuked the winds and the sea, and it became perfectly calm. The men were amazed, and said, 'What kind of a man is this, that even the winds and the sea obey Him?'*

**Matthew 8:26,27 (NASB), Also read: Job 38:22,23 (NASB)**

A recent conversation, sermon and correspondence collided with a March blizzard that dumped as many heavies as snow.

This buffet of happenings brought to mind the "Blizzard of '78" that put The State of New Jersey into a state of emergency and brought our college to a halt...for days.

Joy. Rapture. No classes.

Yet, I learned a lesson as deep as the snow during that week. Even security on campus was having a hard time policing in the midst of those circumstances. Hmmm. Security and out-of-control circumstances seem oxymoron-ish.

What do you do when you can do nothing? You begin to experience life in a slow and focused manner. You are literally trapped. It was as if the Campus Police arrested my pace and confiscated all of life's contrived props as well.

Circumstances do have a way of simply unloading all at once in the same manner as a few inches of snow per hour. Some do what they can to "stay ahead" of the storm, but it's hard to fight it in the middle of its hard winds and incessant pounding.

## PORTAL TO HEAVEN

Life within a blizzard and/or unruly and multiplied circumstances has a way of shoveling a path to the centrality of Christ. When life whites out all or most of our plans, hopes and dreams, we suddenly understand that we have been living "under the circumstances" for too long. Why, oh why, does it take blizzards to figure this out?

*...our citizenship is in heaven. And we eagerly await a Savior from there, the Lord Jesus Christ, who, by the power that enables him to bring everything under his control, will transform our lowly bodies so that they will be like his glorious body.*

**Philippians 3:20,21(NIV). Also: Philippians 6-11,13-21(NIV)**

It was the original "March Madness." Beginning March 9th with drifts up to fifteen-feet high, The Great Blizzard of 1891 was one of the most terrifying storms ever to hit New England. It claimed over 200 lives.

Faced with cabin-fever young men, a YMCA supervisor at a Training School in Springfield, Massachusetts ordered an ordained minister and athletic instructor James Naismith to come up with a safe indoor game to tame the unruly boys.

Two peach baskets, a soccer ball and the original "13 Rules of Basket Ball" were the ingredients Naismith used to create a game that honored the wishes of his boss and fit into the "Muscular Christianity Movement" that Teddy Roosevelt would make famous. Basketball was born.

Naismith spent much of his career mixing faith and athletics through his coaching and other endeavors. He lived to see his game introduced as an Olympic sport. Many of the greatest past and current basketball coaches directly trace their "lineage" to this minister.

## PORTAL TO HEAVEN

Horrific circumstance can actually materialize the deep pre-ordained desires and talents within the believer that turns tragedy into triumph and often changes history. Jesus' approach to the cross began in a "march" toward Jerusalem. His family, some followers and religious leaders thought it madness.

*Now when the time was approaching for Him to be taken up [to heaven], He was determined to go to Jerusalem [to fulfill His purpose].*

**Luke 9:51 (AMP)**
**Also read: Mark 3:20,21,22 (NIV)**

While passing the birthday on March's calendar of my adopted dad, I realized how much I missed taking the late Royal A. Cutler, Jr. to his annual birthday breakfast for his beloved blueberry pancakes.

Our backstory is simple. We had met at church and I asked the recently-retired scientist if he would help me study The Old Testament - a task that seemed overwhelming to me. He agreed. We met weekly and the rest is history. He became my spiritual father and helped show me how scripture plays out in life; and for the better part of thirty years, at that. His anecdotes were like footnotes to The Bible. He was showing me that my life was being written in the same manner as that of the heroes of scripture. No one could make The Word come alive like Royal.

Years later, while writing a newspaper column about seniors who were accomplishing great feats, I thought of crafting a post-mortem tribute about Royal. As I wrote the article, it dawned on me that I was one of Royal's great feats.

No, I was no great student. But he was a great and detailed teacher and took time weekly to disciple me in the nuances of the love of The Father, Son and Holy Spirit. The lessons of scripture jumped off the page and landed in my heart. Through his patience, guidance, compassion and wisdom, I also learned a realm of sonship that could only come through time with a father – the very thing that Old Testament Israel had to learn from their heavenly Father.

## PORTAL TO HEAVEN

One changed life is a great feat. May we pour our life-in-Christ into as many sons and daughters as possible and watch them grow.

*you, Lord, are our Father, our Redeemer from of old is your name.*

**Isaiah 63:16 (NIV)**

Let go and let God...

St. Patrick was kidnapped during his younger years from England and taken to Ireland. During his captivity, he was a shepherd of sorts. Like King David, the effects of the brilliant landscape, wide night skies and being fairly unsheltered through all sorts of weather became the architecture of his soul.

It was during that time that Patrick recognized that the God of his parents was the true God and that he had wasted much time. This lost time seemed to bother him the most.

In a vision, he was told where he could go to board a boat to escape some two hundred miles away. By the end of this epic journey, Patrick was miraculously reunited with his parents in England. They begged him to never leave again.

Again, in a dreamy vision, he saw Irish boys petitioning him to return to Ireland. The Emerald Island eventually became a flock that would listen to their Shepherd and become stalwarts of the gospel.

## PORTAL TO HEAVEN

The great saint acknowledged that somehow God allows the most tragic things to occur in our lives. In Patrick's case, The Omnipotent could have reasoned that exile was the only way to reach the lad. We can't really argue with the results. We can simply "let go and let God."

*'For my thoughts are not your thoughts, neither are your ways my ways,'*
*declares the Lord. 'As the heavens are higher than the earth, so are my ways*
*higher than your ways and my thoughts than your thoughts.'*

**Isaiah 55:8,9 (NIV)**

If St. Pat and I were sitting in a pub, what would the conversation center on?

Perhaps we would exchange cultural jokes over a pint. But after a few beers, men tend to get pretty honest and conversations can go a little deeper. He might tell me of God's mercy upon him during the years following his kidnapping.

Pat might say, "So many favours and graces has the Lord deigned to bestow on me in the land of my captivity. For after chastisement from God, and recognizing him, our way to repay him is to exalt him and confess his wonders before every nation under heaven: For there is no other God, … but God the Father … and his son Jesus Christ, He was made man, conquered death and was received into Heaven … so that every tongue should confess that Jesus Christ is Lord and God, in whom we believe… which makes the believers and the obedient into sons of God and co-heirs of Christ who is revealed, and we worship one God in the Trinity of holy name… And again: 'It is right to reveal and publish abroad the works of God.'" (This quote is from *St. Patrick's Confession*.)

I might sip the Guinness as if sipping the memories of the sins of my youth. Perhaps our tears would drop into the Guinness as we both drank the memory of our chastisement.

## ᴘORTAL ᴛO ʜEAVEN

Back then, Ireland was the farthest land from Pat's upbringing. Today, in a post-modern world, perhaps the barstool is the land of the pagan. I know not. I only know that my "Brother Pat" would go and testify now as he did then over a Guinness here or overseas.

*I consider my life worth nothing to me; my only aim is to finish the race and complete the task the Lord Jesus has given me–the task of testifying to the good news of God's grace.*

**Acts 20:24 (NIV)**

"Let's toast to St. Patrick and his day!"

"So, what exactly am I toasting?" I ask myself.

It is recorded that Patrick was taken prisoner at least twice. Moreover, during his first bout with thieves, pirates and pagans, he was left in the fields as a shepherd to deal with sleet, frost and Ireland's infamous rain on the windswept hills of The Emerald Island. That's an "Achoo" with no one to say "Gesundheit."

During this time, Patrick developed a one-on-one relationship with God and he said that he prayed for hours during every kind of weather. We are talking "marathon man" - not one who offers a little ditty Irish blessing at the beginning of a corn beef and cabbage luncheon. (For further reading, check out the powerful *St. Patrick's Breastplate.*)

In *St. Patrick Confessions*, the saint tells of coming face to face with God in the form of a voice within him. Like Moses and David, this was a shepherd who learned from his flock. The lambs listened to him for their direction and provision and Patrick did the same with his God.

## PORTAL TO HEAVEN

We may love to toast our saints. However, do we want to drink from the same cup that we now raise to them during their celebrations?

*But Jesus answered, 'You do not know what you are asking. Are you able to drink the cup that I am about to drink?' They said to Him, 'We are able.' He said to them, 'My cup you shall drink…'*

**Matthew 20:22,23 (NASB)**

St. Patrick admitted that he never sought God as a boy in England and that his kidnapping as a lad helped capture his soul.

In St. Patrick's Confession, he tells of connecting with God through the lonely times of shepherding during his exile.

"But after I came to Ireland—every day I had to tend sheep, and many times a day I prayed—the love of God and His fear came to me more and more, and my faith was strengthened. And my spirit was moved so that in a single day I would say as many as a hundred prayers, … and this even when I was staying in the woods and on the mountains; and I used to get up for prayer before daylight, through snow, through frost, through rain, and I felt no harm, and there was no sloth in me—as I now see, because the spirit within me was then fervent."

## PORTAL TO HEAVEN

God will allow us to be alone and/or in difficult situations. In that quiet, it is easier to hear Him. Whether inadvertent isolation or imprisonment like Joseph of the Old Testament or a deliberate choice whereby Jesus "would withdraw to desolate places and pray," we get to hear without distraction. In Patrick and Joseph's cases, they were not only without distraction, they were without opportunity.

Is it possible that great opportunities and ease of circumstance could put us in danger of wandering like one of St. Pat's sheep and lead to a separation from The Great Shepherd?

*But Jesus often withdrew to lonely places and prayed…*

**Luke 5:16 (NIV)**
**Also read: Deuteronomy 8:3, 10-14**

The reason we admire people we've termed "saints" is because of their utter resolve to serve Christ. Usually, their lives were so immersed in His character and service and their hearts so marked by thankfulness, that *each day* propelled them toward their savior. Have we grown so soft that we can't even reserve *one day* to honor their true memory?

After escaping from his kidnappers, he returned to his home only to answer God's call to go back to Ireland to spread the gospel and save souls. Like Jesus, he leaves the security and love of home in order to go give his life to pagans and ignorant men.

How could we reduce such love to leprechauns and green beer that are so far removed from the very man we say we are celebrating?

## ϷORTAL ᏟO ϤEAVEN

Saints like Patrick open up portals to heaven as we study, and celebrate, their unflinching mindset to live *each day* like their savior.

So wear a shamrock because Patrick used it as a symbol of The Trinity. Raise a beer if you can also raise the standard here and use the toast as a way of corralling the conversation toward the bravery of this determined, and adopted, "Irishman."

*The Spirit of the Lord is on Me, because He has anointed Me to preach good news to the poor. ...Do not get drunk...which leads to reckless indiscretion. Instead, be filled with the Spirit. Luke 4:18,19*

**(BSB), Ephesians 5:18 (BSB)**

"She laughs at the future."

"Laugh?"That's a laugh.

I don't know who *she* is, but I'd love to pick her brains about that little quote.

Where does *she* get off being so giddy about college loans, offspring, marriage, school taxes and those smaller issues like nuclear threat and dirty bombs down at the end of my street?

I googled *she* and found her secret. *She* is too busy to worry about the future. *She* is working hard every day on behalf of her family and her husband.

There is a sense that her work will pay off whether or not there is a dirty bomb being made down the street. In fact, *she* may walk right by where such evil spins its web and not notice because *she* is on her way to help the needy on that same street.

## PORTAL TO HEAVEN

*She* is anticipation. She bases such confidence on her experience of God's faithfulness to her. *She* does her best and lets God do the rest... including the foiling of those who mess with dirty bombs.

*Who can find a virtuous woman? For her price is far above rubies.*

**Proverbs 31:10 (KJV)  Also read: Proverbs 31:11-31**

The uncomfortable aspect of paradox does not make it any less of a reality.

When we think of the concept of anticipation, is it always one of rapturous joy, unmitigated eagerness and childlike "Are we there yet?"

Actually, anticipation can carry the weight of the wait. We "anxiously await" is the clearest juxtaposition of the idea that life is full of tension between two seemingly opposing ideas.

"Anxiously" could be filled with anxiety. "Await" could be full of expectation. How do they coexist? Ah, but they do.

There is a scripture that says that we should consider trials pure joy. To the naked eye, that might seem an optical delusion rather than an optical illusion. Yet, we respect this as absolute truth.

There is something in us that desires these lines of life to be less blurred so we don't need eyeglasses of faith. We do not want paradox, juxtaposition, irony, oxymoron or any other thing that creates tension. In essence, we want God to line up the stars as if they were a personal stairway to heaven.

## ₽ORTAL ₲O ⱧEAVEN

There is a loveliness to the childlike trust we are commended to maintain - especially during the "anxiously" part of the "await."

*My soul, wait thou only upon God; for my expectation is from Him…In the morning, Lord, You hear my voice; in the morning I lay my requests before You and wait in expectantly… 'I'm on my way! I'll be there soon!' Yes! Come, Master Jesus! Amen.*

**Psalm 62:5 (KJV), Psalm 5:3 (NIV), Revelation 22:20 (The Message)**

"Why does the earth keep going around and around? What is the meaning of the sunrise?

God is God. He certainly could have made the world flat with an absence of spinning so we wouldn't get so dizzy trying to explain gravity and other great mysteries.

To anticipate the sunrise can be a glorious experience – especially on a daily basis.

Sure, the world's 24-hour revolutions are easy for God. But for a lot of the world, it's an everyday grind to scrape up enough rice or bread or whatever for their "daily flour."

So, what's with this sunrise?

For us yawners foolish enough to gaze at the eastern horizon, there is a miracle-metaphor that's a little hard to miss. If the world were flat, it would be difficult to notice this second-chance, resurrection, new-life symbol while standing on a floating earth in the shape of a piece of toast. No, God knows what He's doing.

## PORTAL TO HEAVEN

God hires out the sun like He sent His Son. It's so bright we shield our eyes and yet are still drawn to see it the very moment it appears.

So this symbol is not just for the hope of every calendar day. It's also about the anticipation for that day when we'll look to the east and we'll see The Son and everything will be new…and all without a strong cup of Joe.

*The steadfast love of the Lord never ceases; his mercies never come to an end; they are new every morning; great is your faithfulness.*

**Lamentations 3:22,23 (ESV)**

## "I Got Nuthin…'"

"The doldrums" is a term originating from the maritime experience of sailing for days or weeks without wind. Since it often happened near the equator, you can add heat to this awful experience.

All of the anticipation of getting to shore suddenly comes to a grinding halt. Captains and their sailors would have gone bonkers if they had forgotten to bring the newest novel by Twain or Dickens. There might have been those lucky few who memorized The New Testament while sweating to death. When life is as listless as the doldrums are for seamen, it is not unusual to go down the slippery slope of losing hope.

We sip our coffee at Starbucks and sadly tell our best friend, "I got nuthin'."

How in the world does life hit the brakes? Moreover, what if our life is in the shop for years?

The weight of the wait has only one purpose. It forces us to beg God for answers as we acknowledge that we don't have all of the solutions we thought we did. It also forces even the non-mechanic to look under the hood.

## PORTAL TO HEAVEN

During the doldrums, it's natural to look up for the wind. Even if it's to blame God for a lack of wind, we do find ourselves looking up. And that's just the start.

*But he said to me, 'My grace is sufficient for you, for my power is made perfect in weakness.' Therefore I will boast all the more gladly about my weaknesses, so that Christ's power may rest on me.*

**2 Corinthians 12:9 (NIV)**

After witnessing several years of presidential primary and general-election debates, I am now convinced that there are perfect people who, according to themselves, never make mistakes. Unfortunately, I am not one of them.

As a Christian, I have this top-secret vexation that I am not only imperfect, but I can't even get close to becoming like the only perfect one: Jesus. "Holy Frustration, Batman!"

The reason this is a little freaky is because those who know Jesus as their God are actually promised that they will be like Christ. There is a long time between receiving this as a promise and receiving this promise.

What's a person to do? Sit and anticipate? No. We are responsible for more than patient waiting or even well-meaning holy frustration.

This interim period between the promise and the promise-received is known as "sanctification" or "Spring Training" as the theologians call it. While we won't hurry this glorious end through more-and-more spiritual push-ups, we can certainly cooperate by learning and practicing the ways of Christ.

## PORTAL TO HEAVEN

At first, we may perceive Jesus to be a tough coach. And yet, it's better than learning the lying ways so skillfully practiced in political debates by those who already think they've attained perfection.

*Don't copy the behavior and customs of this world, but let God transform you into a new person by changing the way you think. Then you will learn to know God's will for you, which is good and pleasing and perfect.*

**Romans 12:2 (NIV)**
**Also read: John 14:15 (NIV), 2 Corinthians 3:1 (NIV), Hebrews 12:2 (NIV)**

Nails are the literal and metaphorical representation of what holds a house together.

While the beginning of every house is land, foundation and lumber, its actual genesis lies in the dream behind the structure. Our dream was a historic house high on a hill overlooking The Hudson River. It was built and owned by The Knickerbocker Ice Company. The home was strategically perched so that the owners could view the work of the ice cutters who were carving blocks of ice to ship to Manhattan.

On the other hand, my house of birth was built by my father who was wrestling with the living needs a large family.

After the seventh baby came, we moved into a 15-room, three-story Victorian by means of necessity as Mom hardly had enough room to change a diaper in the other house.

In "The Color Green," songwriter Rich Mullins spoke beautifully of the earth as a house: "And I'm amazed when I remember Who it was that built this house."

From the earth's rotation never skipping a beat to photosynthesis to unnumbered galaxies to gravity to the atmosphere, it has been observed that all of this was constructed so that man could survive and prosper and grow to know that his architect did all of this in the manner that I once prepared a nursery for our baby.

## PORTAL TO HEAVEN

Scripture refers to the body as a home. When we look upon the cross of Christ, we see that our "houses" are held together by nails.

*For every house is built by someone, but God is the builder of everything…*
*Our body is the house in which our spirit lives here on earth.*

**Hebrews 3:4 (NIV), 2 Corinthians 5:1 (WEB)**

"Pain comes knocking at every door." That's a phrase no one wants to think about. There comes a time when it seems like it's just our hurt living under boarded up shack held together by some rusted nails.

Suffering knocks. We reluctantly open the door, shack or mansion, and let it in.

The amazing thing about the Lenten season is that it helps us fix our attention on the suffering of Christ. If we use our imaginations, we can get more out of scripture than just words.

Luke, the master of detail, chooses only six words to adhere Jesus to the cross: "...they nailed him to the cross." That's it. Within the context of his entire passion, one would think that the nails deserve more specifics. But no, it's left to our imagination.

It is good for us to ponder. This identity with his pain drives home the notion that He truly understands our trials. If this is true, shouldn't the partial result of our suffering steer us toward empathy?

## PORTAL TO HEAVEN

Wretched sufferings are some of the nails that hold us together – a basic bond of humanity. Whether it's the pain of those who seem like a galaxy away or someone as close as a household member or friend, invite yourself over to their shack or mansion for a cup of suffering. That will be a knock that they'll be glad to answer.

*Remember that your Christian brothers and sisters all over the world are going through the same kind of suffering you are...*

**1 Peter 5:9 (NLT)**

**Also read: 2 Corinthians 1:3-5 (BSB)**

In short, portals to heaven are observed through our senses as "the presence of God in the present."

One sure way to a portal is by slowing down our reading and literally using our fingernails to point to one word at a time in The Bible. Place yourself in the narrative.

Lent is a good time for this technique. Slowly observe Jesus and the character and action of the disciples.

It is easy to take potshots at the apostles - thinking of them as spiritual weaklings and perhaps silently injecting, "I would have been braver or smarter." Ha, ha. What a joke.

It's not until we truly see the reality of their "present" that portals to heaven can open up through scriptures. The Holy Spirit uses our imagination to take us where our fingernails cannot.

For instance, the disciples had attached themselves to a star. Jesus was popular. He was doing miracles. They were in his shadow. They were the "in crowd." They were taken care of. Things were peachy and secure.

All of a sudden, things turned on a dime. It would have been like losing your house to the bank, a cancer diagnosis, a spouse dying, an employer downsizing last Friday afternoon, a betrayal by a best friend and so on.

## PORTAL TO HEAVEN

These "dumb" apostles, unlike us of course, had attached themselves to the wrong Christ and it left them hanging... by their fingernails.

*And He began to teach them that the Son of Man must suffer many things...*

**Read: Mark 8:31-35 (NIV)**

If you were having your last supper on earth with friends or family or both, what would be the last words you'd like to nail down? ... Ah, hmm. Clear the throat. Ready...

"I'd like to raise a cup to all of you. You have shown me love. You have stood by me in my trials. I can only hope that you have received love from me..." Ching-ching go the wine glasses. Or something like that.

But what if you heard a lot of murmuring in the middle of your speech? Upon listening closer, you thought you heard some arguments going on about who was considered your greatest friend and who did the most for you. "Oh boy," you'd think, "I'm not going to see them again and they are not even listening to my toast. Did I invite the wrong people?"

Scripture says that Jesus longed for this last supper - this very special Passover meal. And what he heard and saw was positioning. Of course, we would never do such a thing.

## ℘ORTAL ℑO ℌEAVEN

Jesus revealed through example and symbols that serving His followers was tantamount to serving His Father; that heaven lives to serve. While they were brownnosing Christ in order for a better seat, they were actually mistreating each other by missing the very point of the bread, wine and the basin and towel.

Even when we talk-over God and position ourselves, Jesus still gets the last word. You might say, Jesus nailed it...permanently.

*Now there was also a dispute among them, as to which of them should be considered the greatest...*

**Read: Luke 22:24-30**

I was rolling away the stone. It's not that I'm Jesus' advance man. It's for the Easter display out on our road.

"OOL!" That's "Ouch Out Loud." I got the nastiest splinter on that faux plywood "boulder." Oh, did that smart! Half the "Ouch" was in the irony of how much that little splinter hurt – a far cry from nails going through a wrist.

Christ didn't fall off the cross. The nails did their job.

Properly used, nails will always do the job. In fact, I have often pulled out nails, straightened them out and used them a second time. They can hold an entire house or building together. Nails are a pretty determined piece of hardware.

That firmness reminds us of the cross and of the love of Jesus. He fastens himself to the splintered and broken lumber of our souls and somehow creates a home that can be lived in and shared. Some of our wood is rough-cut and other pieces have been infested by tiny critters that make even big-boys cry.

Without his nails, our lives are a house of cards. Nails are so hard that they can penetrate or override the wood. You can find nails after a house burns down.

## PORTAL TO HEAVEN

Christ has steel-like love. A secondary portal is how even a small, but determined, piece of forgiveness can pierce the hardest wood. One "tiny" act of forgiveness can roll away someone's stone – even when that act incites an "OOL" from our lips.

*He upholds the universe by the word of his power. After making purification for sins, he sat down at the right hand of the Majesty on high.*

**Hebrews 1:3 (ESV)**
**Also read: Colossians 1:17 (NASB)**

# PEN YOUR PORTALS

# April

## PORTALS TO HEAVEN

God creates a new day by simply spinning the globe the way a Globetrotter spins a basketball on his finger: effortlessly.

By continuing the longest spinning streak in history, the earth rotates around every twenty-four hours while at the same time circling the sun. The world has no big block-motor or dual carburetors and yet we mark time and days by this engine that propels us into our personal and global future. But what is God's purpose in this machine that never runs out of gas nor gets flat tires nor needs a pit stop?

When we see the sun, we see a new chance. Though we have a calendar that gives us hints as to what the day will bring, we cannot know all of today's "new" wealth until we've accumulated it. Some of that wealth may come through mistakes or sin and yet God will even use that as a deposit.

It's beneficial to picture the earth on that continuous run around the sun rather than just seeing the sun sneak up over the horizon because then we see each day as thrusting our trust and pushing us toward a greater goal – and this often includes when we get some bad fuel of disappointments in ourselves and others.

It's dangerous for us to measure our days within either the constructs of our limited imagination and knowledge or, worse yet, our fears of tomorrow's spin.

## PORTAL TO HEAVEN

Our Globetrotter God knows how to put a positive spin on our lives.

*The faithful love of the Lord never ends! His mercies never cease. Great is his faithfulness; His mercies begin afresh each morning.*

**Lamentations 3:22,23 (NLT)**

I was traveling down the highway near my home when I realized I was driving under a canopy of lime green leaves.

In just one day, trees came forth and announced that Spring was not retreating. Hallelujah! I pulled in my driveway and noticed that the lamppost garden and the edging of my little white well house had come alive with that long-anticipated yellow burst...daffodils!

Why does life change so fast? Does God put a premium on shock-value? Or is it simply a down payment on a promise?

When Spring suddenly trumpets its arrival through its cone-shaped daffodils and the trees look as if an artist exchanged a winter-scene canvas for a fully-developed painting of May, there is a portal to heaven so bright and clear that it screams of just how new "new" can be.

This portends an eternal Spring where newness will be as shocking every moment as when we first laid our eyes on Christ and His heaven. Can I imagine such newness? No. I cannot think up something I cannot Google or ask about or stir up in my mind. No one has ever returned with a front-page scoop to assure me.

## PORTAL TO HEAVEN

A promise is, in itself, new. But just as I step on the gas pedal on that highway that leads to my house, I realize that it's a mesmerizing metaphor of this journey on earth that leads to my new home.

*And God will wipe away every tear from their eyes; there shall be no more death, nor sorrow, nor crying. There shall be no more pain, for the former things have passed away. Then He who sat on the throne said, 'Behold, I make all things new.' And He said to me, 'Write, for these words are true and faithful.'*

**Revelation 21:4,5 (NKJV). Editor's emphasis.**

If you were told that you would someday meet someone who would change your life, you might stay up all night wondering who this person is and why they would become so significant.

You might even be on the lookout every time you walked into a restaurant. Before you would meet this person, your life would be centered on your responsibilities. However, having a child or being involved in a child's life, changes everything.

We can't conjure up their exact personalities, interests, soft-spots, temperament, precise hair color or their height no less the idiosyncracies that seem to explode during adolescence or the richness of that relationship as an adult child.

It would all be too "new." However, once in our hearts, we can't imagine life without them…

On my way into a restaurant, I met two young men in the valet lot. As they handed me my ticket, I asked them if they had ever met Jesus. In that brief exchange, I found it hard to explain how that one relationship with Christ changed everything in my life.

## PORTAL TO HEAVEN

There is a privilege and weight to knowing that you or I could be the one person who changes another's life by introducing them to Jesus who changes everything forever.

*The first thing Andrew did was to find his brother Simon and tell him, 'We have found the Messiah' (that is, the Christ)…The next day John saw Jesus coming toward him, and said, 'Behold! The Lamb of God who takes away the sin of the world!'*

**John 1:41 (NIV), John 1:29 (NKJV)**

Growing up near the Jersey shore, I was exposed to the Atlantic Ocean many times.

I used to close my eyes when I went under the water and felt the exhilaration as I popped my head back up after the wave broke over me.

The Atlantic was so vast. I would imagine England out there somewhere. On the surface, it was a forever-green body that had its own personality and temper if you "crossed it."

We also belonged to a swim club. I would keep my eyes open under water and loved to pick up a quarter or whatever on the bottom of the pool. My brothers and I used to swim to the bottom, squat and pretend to be playing cards for as long as we could hold our breadth.

Much later in life, I learned to snorkel. It blended the swim club and ocean experience into one. My eyes were open to the "schools" of choreography. Scuba diving takes it many steps further; you feel like an invited guest of the undersea.

Newness is sometimes right below the surface. I missed what was swimming right around my feet in The Atlantic.

## PORTAL TO HEAVEN

With some tools and a little instruction, God can reveal what's below the surface – whether that's The Atlantic, the people right in front of me or the unfathomable riches of His goodness, character or promises.

*I pray that the eyes of your heart may be enlightened, so that you will know what is the hope of His calling, what are the riches of the glory of His inheritance in the saints...*

**Ephesians 1:18 (NASB)**

As far as discovery, surprise and inventing go, it would be cool to get Leonardo Da Vinci, Louis Pasteur, Isaac Newton, Thomas Edison and Albert Einstein in one room like a "Dream Team" and see what they'd come up with...

All great thinkers build on previous concepts, experiments and inventions. Even in law, precedents are established that set a "new" order of law. Wouldn't it be something if we could "build" off the mind of God? "But we have the mind of Christ" according to scripture. (1 Corinthians 2:16b)

One of the more remarkable concepts in The Bible is that we have been given The Holy Spirit. He is equal-part God and resides within and He will guide us into all truth. It doesn't mean we'll end up ranking with Da Vinci, but it could mean that we have more at our disposal than we ever imagined.

## PORTAL TO HEAVEN

The Holy Spirit is for my life - not Einstein's life. It's not just a matter of faith, but a matter of moment-by-moments where I honestly address the question: "Am I allowing The Holy Spirit enough room to speak and lead in the moment or am I talking over Him and stepping on His feet?" It's sort of like Edison clearing the counter in his lab and stating, "I tired of my old way and I must start anew."

'What no eye has seen, what no ear has heard, and what no human mind has conceived'—the things God has prepared for those who love him—these are the things God has revealed to us by his Spirit. The Spirit searches all things, even the deep things of God. For who knows a person's thoughts except their own spirit within them? In the same way no one knows the thoughts of God except the Spirit of God. What we have received is not the spirit of the world, but the Spirit who is from God, so that we may understand what God has freely given us.

**| 1 Corinthians 2:9-12 (NIV)**

Looking outside, it's easy to observe that life is changing. Spring is a clear metaphor that I haven't kept pace with those changes. This could be something as insignificant as my clothes or as profound as my career.

Dull. It's who I would be if someone didn't push me.

That Someone is God. He didn't make me to be a couch-potato boiling on the stove of numbness until the windows steam up and I don't even notice that the snow has melted.

Spring shouts!

It refuses normality.

Clever God that He is, He disguises His alarm clock as crocuses, forsythia, daffodils and a much more tender wind. He camouflages school as budding light green leaves, tulips and apple blossoms. He hides push-ups and sit-ups within verdant fields and flowering crabapple trees.

He could make all of the changes that He is working within us drudgery so that our resistance would be all the more justified. But He does not. He is the kindest-hardest boot camp sergeant.

## ᑭORTAL ᏩTO ᏂEAVEN

Spring pushes its way into our consciousness. It brings change and progression. One thing leads to another and it shouts, "Growth is imperative." A seed in a garden turns into a tomato plant. An empty field magically produces "Knee-high-by-July" corn. Players go from Spring camp to champs.

*Take pains with these things; be absorbed in them, so that your progress will be evident to all.*

**1 Timothy 4:15 (NAS)**

Spring is like going to an NBA game as a little guy and marveling at the three-pointers, precision passing and gutsy rebounds. The young boy thinks, "I'm going to be a professional basketball player."

NBA All-Star Paul Westphal once answered a question from a seventh-grader regarding what it takes to "spring" into professional basketball: "What was it like to be an NBA all-star and play in All-Star game?"

Without hesitation, the famous shooting and point guard replied: "When I was young, my older brothers would beat me up pretty good on the court. But, then I learned how to beat them. Later, I made the high school team and worked very hard. Before long, I was playing college and practicing every day to get better. At one point, I made it to the NBA. I did well, pushing myself at every practice. Then, one day, I stepped on the court of an NBA All-Star game. Being an All-Star was a result of practicing and improving and advancing my game each day that I played. That's what it's like to be an NBA All-Star."

I doubt that was the answer the seventh-grader was expecting.

## PORTAL TO HEAVEN

Young fans may think flawless three-point shots just come without cost. But that is like the person passing by a flower garden that has taken years of painstaking care and casually remarking without breaking their stride, "Oh, isn't The Spring lovely?"

*...unless a kernel of wheat falls to the ground and dies, it remains only a single seed. But if it dies, it produces many seeds. Anyone who loves their life will lose it, while anyone who hates their life in this world will keep it for eternal life.*

**John 12:24,25 (NIV)**

Springtime is the evidence of things that were not seen during winter.

Buying a box of seeds is spending money for a promise of "stored energy." It's not until germination takes place that there is some kind of proof of worth.

But it's the actual "clock" of the seed that's fascinating. Germination reminds me of our cellular clock which ticks and ticks and no man has ever tricked. Even Jesus himself aged as part of God's plan for us to see His human-side growth. While scientists today explore the "germination" of our bodies and why aging through "cellular senescence" occurs, we are faced with our inescapable "dead-line."

God is both the gardener and the scientist of the soul. He has set eternity in the heart of man and that clock will never stop ticking. Seeds may not be able to decide as to whether to grow into an eternal being worthy of the glory of heaven, but humans have been given that choice.

Metaphorically, the germination of the soul plods forward through the frozen-ground months and the winters we weather and the mounds of dirt over us that feel like the weight of death.

## PORTAL TO HEAVEN

For those who choose Christ, we are growing and transforming even when we can't observe it - and God-forbid that another make judgments about what they cannot see in us!

*Therefore we do not lose heart. Though outwardly we are wasting away, yet inwardly we are being renewed day by day.*

**2 Corinthians 4:16 (NIV)**
**Also read: Psalm 37:25,26 (KJV)**

Drooping Daffodils.

In nature, Spring represents one of the shortest windows of ecstasy. One minute, a crocus renews all hope. A few weeks later, it's gone. One day, the lilac tree captures all my senses and makes me want to sell perfume. Before long, it looks like a big green bush with some wimpy lavender-yellow ends.

It was in the deep of Summer when my gaze transfixed on the front entrance of my sister's New Jersey shore home. Family members were coming in and out trying to hold beach towels, coolers and kids without dropping any one of them.

As I stared at her front door, it dawned on me that this would one day come to an end. Time doesn't sit still. It made me want to enjoy that summer day for all it was worth.

I sat across from a man at dinner that survived a serious spinal cancer operation. He told me that he was thankful for every day that he could stand up. As he walked away, he admonished me, "Find some gratitude." As if to make sure I heard him, he looked over his shoulder and repeated himself, "Find some gratitude, man."

## PORTAL TO HEAVEN

Spring's transient beauty is a metaphor of the passing appointments of this life. We are to enjoy and be utterly grateful for those things God has placed in front of us...now. My sister eventually sold that beloved shore home.

*You should enjoy every day of your life, no matter how long you live. But remember that you will die, and you will be dead much longer than you were alive. And after you are dead, you cannot do anything.*

**Ecclesiastes 11:8 (ERV)**

When I was a little league pitcher, a rainy April day would be the most depressing part of my week – especially if it also washed out the Mets games as well as mine. Even if it cleared up, the field would probably be too soggy to play.

Weekend warriors live for a sunny Saturday and when it doesn't come, it could throw off their schedule for weeks as they watch their grass turn into hayfields and their gardens resemble mulch soup.

Then, there is an old saying that farmers use: "A dry Spring will scare you, but a wet Spring will starve you." When life rains on our parade, our attitudes can get a little waterlogged and our prayers may seem to get washed away.

If our hearts are as fickle as the weather, then circumstance rules our minds. We can be tempted to think that God or fate is working against us.

## PORTAL TO HEAVEN

Reservoirs finally fill up, California lifts their water ban, "April showers bring May flowers" and hayfields can finally grow. Moreover, some Little Leaguers and your favorite baseball club can use an extra day's rest.

*Your unfailing love, O LORD, is as vast as the heavens; your faithfulness reaches beyond the clouds… He reached down from on high and took hold of me; he drew me out of deep waters… Trust in the Lord with all your heart. Never rely on what you think you know… And we know that in all things God works for the good of those who love him, who have been called according to his purpose… You make me lie down during rainouts.*

**Psalm 36:5 (NLT), Psalm 18:16 (NIV), Proverbs 3:5 (GNT), Romans 8:28 (NIV)**

**Psalm 23:2 (RJLGV or RJL Goof Ver.)**

Whenever I'd confess sinfulness to my pastor, he'd put his hand on my shoulder and say, "It's just God peeling another layer of the onion." I understood his analogy all too well. I'd literally run out of my kitchen whenever I chopped them – even in the dead of winter.

I tried different things to mask the burning pain of onions. Chop them certain ways. Wait until the very last second so I wouldn't have to repeat this painful process on the second half. Delay or no delay, my eyes would tear so badly it would delay the completion of my tomato sauce every time. But, oh, the taste of sauce on that pasta was worth it.

It's analogous to working through pain versus ignoring it to get to victory. The same thing goes for emotions. While many folks never shed a tear, I really don't trust myself when I don't cry. If the wound is deep enough, I will cry. But that's the trick: How deep is deep enough to get my attention?

Scripture talks about the God who "bottles tears." It has many implications. God relates and feels my pain. He's aware of self-inflicted hurts caused by my sin and the injury to me when sinned against by "enemies." I can also be sure to leave my pain with Him instead of carrying it around. I can know that he keeps records of wrongs. This list could be an endless compilation of God's fairness and awareness.

## PORTAL TO HEAVEN

God takes the time to capture AND bottle tears. I may run out of the kitchen. But shouldn't I at least deliberate on why I'm shivering out there during this deja-vu exercise?

*You have taken account of my wanderings; Put my tears in Your bottle. Are they not in Your book?*

**Psalm 56:8 (NASB) Also read: Psalm 43:5 (NIV)**

# Did You Cry on The Cross?

Did You cry on the cross
Or were they all spent
From the moment you were sent?
Did You cry on the cross?
I know the women did
Thinking about their loss.

Did You cry on the cross?
There's no account that You did.
Were tears all in heaven hid?
Did You cry on the cross
Over the pathetic me's
Who didn't recognize their boss?

Did You cry on the cross?
You internalized all pain -
That was part of the cost.
No, I never saw You cry.
You were too busy dying.
I am the one who cries.

**© 2016, Robert J. LaCosta.**

What good are tears?

At my lowest points, either privately or in the company of trusted friends, I have let a river of sorrow flow in a manner like a reservoir whose dam had been broken in pieces.

I wondered then and I wonder now where those droplets went. Did they oh-so-slowly empty into The Sea of Suffering where they swelled with the remnants of tragedy and pain of unknown compatriots?

When a child cries, it can be a knee-jerk to something that overwhelms them. But there are other times when they are simply trying to get the attention of the nearest adult who will assure them that they are not alone in their pain.

Could that be the purpose of tears? It's as if I cry, "Is there anyone out there? Does anyone understand the way I feel? Will there come an end to all of this?"

## PORTAL TO HEAVEN

I want to know that someone is walking along the Sea of Suffering and knows its every wave very well.

*During the days of Jesus' life on earth, he offered up prayers and petitions with fervent cries and tears to the one who could save him from death, and he was heard because of his reverent submission. Son though he was, he learned obedience from what he suffered and, once made perfect, he became the source of eternal salvation for all who obey him and was designated by God to be high priest in the order of Melchizedek.*

**Hebrews 5:7-10 (NIV)**

"Sticks and stones may break my bones, but names will never hurt me."

What this sing-songy rhyme intimates is that the unseen can't hurt. Only a child could believe that.

Because we don't see others' wounds, we often ask, "What is wrong with that person?"

If I were writing a sci-fi movie, I might show a man or woman walking around with all these daggers thrust into the heart, back, head, and all over. An extra problem is when we go to hug them and our daggers bump into theirs and the clanging attempt causes an awkward space between our bodies.

The unseen hurts often come through unseen weapons and the chief culprit is the tongue. I knew a woman who would be laughing one second and killing you the next with the most serrated-edged-knife mouth that ripped as much coming out as it did going in.

Getting back to my sci-fi movie, I might add that the dagger has a poison tip with a serum of memory liquid that flows around and around the body in an incessant loop of torture.

## ᑭORTAL ᑕTO ᕼEAVEN

This happens to us and from us. Because of the unseen and dangerous world of words, we have seven billion people walking around with invisible hurts. "God only knows" might be appropriate here. May He forgive us for our part and show us the unseen that we might use words to carefully pull out some daggers and apply some balm.

*Set a guard over my mouth, LORD; keep watch over the door of my lips...*

**Psalm 141:3 (NIV)**

**Also read: Proverbs 12:18 (NLT), James 3:3-12 (NIV)**

This is no daydream or nightmare...I covertly glance around. There it is. How can I reach it without anyone noticing? I look over my shoulder. I slowly and cautiously slide my left hand down to my pocket. Oh no. It's not there. I try the same sly maneuver toward the right pocket. Mercy! It's there.

Tissues. I'm reaching for Kleenex and this drama is real.

Whether it's hoping the mucous won't get ahead of the tissues during a counseling session or subtly going for some in my pocket during worship or another emo-moment, I find myself in this recurring position of wiping away tears.

Life is a drama. I truly am thankful for all of those counselors who are adept at preparing for pain and its release; who deftly place tissue boxes within arms-reach.

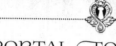

## PORTAL TO HEAVEN

God had a giant-sized hanky wrapped around the ripped muscular tissues of Jesus. He left that cloth behind in the tomb to remind us that He is always within arms-reach. The humble sinner wraps himself in this linen of forgiveness so he might be raised with Him. God goes one better than understanding our pain. He has promised that there will be one final tissue. With it, He will wipe away every tear. There will be no more suffering and that includes the pain of remembering all hurts.

Knowing this, a tissue box will never look the same to me.

*He will wipe away every tear from their eyes, and death shall be no more, neither shall there be mourning, nor crying, nor pain anymore, for the former things have passed away.*

**Revelation 21:4 (ESV)**

"Rainy days and Mondays always get me down" were some famous musical lyrics at one time.

Songwriters enjoy the easy refrains of rain because it rhymes with pain and is drenched in symbolism. And what good tragic movie director fails to include pelts of rain during the lover's break-up or the heart-wrenching death scene?

And for what purpose does God employ this metaphor of rain in the song and story of our lives?

At more than one wedding or party, we've been forced inside due to inclement weather. The fellowship was actually sweeter because people were physically closer, chairs were right next to each other and no one could wander on a distant walk. The rain indirectly connected us.

Pain has a way of doing the same thing. If we never experienced the drizzle, showers and the absolute downpours of life, just how would we know how to offer someone our umbrella?

## PORTAL TO HEAVEN

Rain has a way of getting our attention. In rain's most memorable and ironic role, the skies eternally opened up when The Maker of Rain cleared the air by taking every pelt from heaven. In Jesus, God stooped down to offer me His "umbrella."

*Praise be to the God and Father of our Lord Jesus Christ, the Father of compassion and the God of all comfort, who comforts us in all our troubles, so that we can comfort those in any trouble with the comfort we ourselves receive from God.*

**2 Corinthians 1:3,4 (NIV)**

**Also read: John 16:33, Luke 23:44,45, Isaiah 60:2**

A lot of us have developed the awful life-habit of looking down - at cell phones, that is.

Things are different for me now. I look up a lot.

Ever since I began to dabble in the dirt with some flowers, I'm suddenly interested in rain. Figuring out a watering schedule can be laughable without a weather app.

I'm not alone.

"Everyone talks about the weather, but nobody does anything about it and climate is what we expect, weather is what we get," Mark Twain quipped, probably in part from his experience with his gardens at his huckleberry home in Hartford.

Gardens aren't the only mouths open for a drink. Getting pool water to the perfect height is important for proper skimming and filtration. It gets me looking up when the water is down.

I've become more comfortable with rain and even enjoy walking in it although I have not yet graduated to singing in it with apologies to Gene Kelly. I even miss the showers when they don't come.

## ᴩORTAL ᴳTO ᴴEAVEN

Rain's necessity showers us with spiritual analogy. No, we don't look up and ask God to rain trials down on us. But when the tests come, we know it's all part of making the garden of our souls bloom.

*Consider it all joy, my brethren, when you encounter various trials, knowing that the testing of your faith produces endurance.*

**James 1:2,3 (NASB)**

Why have rain-effects phone apps become so popular? Is it because the unwanted noise of traffic, airplanes, intrusive overhead music and the like is forcing us to enjoy silence or some soothing sound instead?

For the tinnitus sufferer, however, there is no escape from noise. Tinnitus is literally sound emanating from within the head. Its sounds can range from ocean waves, steam pressure, tones, beeping, crickets, buzzing or even a song. One patient heard "Silent Night" over and over.

Since there is no known cure, health care professionals usually tell the poor souls to "mask" the annoying problem by listening to other sounds so as to distract the brain from concentrating or obsessing with it. Many hearing aids now include maskers. The most popular sound is water whether it is ocean waves, babbling brooks or a gentle rain.

In the spiritual realm, we all hear the "tinnitus" of Satan. He constantly prods us to relive or regret the past, bring to mind the frustration of besetting sins and barrage us with accusations. His oldest trick in The Book is recorded in Genesis in The Garden of Eden: he lies about God.

## PORTAL TO HEAVEN

God uses heavenly sounds in the form of His Word to drown out the noise of hell. But like tinnitus sufferers, we have to turn on our "masker" – The Bible.

*...whatever is true, whatever is noble, whatever is right, whatever is pure, whatever is lovely, whatever is admirable—if anything is excellent or praiseworthy—think about such things.*

**Philippians 4:8 (NIV)**

**Also read: 2 Corinthians 10:5**

It is said that there is an ebb and flow to life. We tell kids to be patient. We encourage friends waiting for the flow when the ebb seems to have the upper hand. We quote, "This, too, shall pass."

When relationships, finances, dreams and circumstance seem to "teem" up in life's downpour, we find that we need the same counsel that we dispense.

But there is a higher counsel from which rain descends.

Sometimes, this can pelt and sting our senses so that we want nothing more than to get out of the rain. At other times, it's just a drizzle and, though we're caught out in it, it provides a gentler awakening.

Like the nursery rhyme, we may want to say, "Rain, rain, go away, come again some other day." But such procrastination wouldn't work anyway.

Perhaps it's just better when we take our own advice for rain because it plays a great part in this ebb and flow.

There will come a time, and probably soon enough, when we'll be wishing for more flow and not so much ebb.

## PORTAL TO HEAVEN

Trust the above-sequenced flow of precipitation and try splashing in heaven's puddles when needed.

*I know what it is to be in need, and I know what it is to have plenty. I have learned the secret of being content in any and every situation...*

**Philippians 4:12 (NIV)**

Someone said he had gone to six wakes and funerals in the last few weeks and he's not even a clergyman or an undertaker.

That's pretty much a snapshot of life's weather as stated in the proverb, "When it rains, it pours." We wish we knew why.

We look to weather as a mentor of sorts. For example, there's an incredible recurring and dramatic scenario that plays out around our east-facing home. We regularly get to see the storms shaping up that commonly come from the west.

We position ourselves on the front or side porch and wait for the downpour. After it begins to clear, we race to the backyard with camera in hand and there it is, voila, a great rainbow that has bragging rights over the storm.

No one wants to make light of the meteorological metaphors of lives although there is irony that living creatures make The Obituaries the most popular page in newspapers.

## ᕭORTAL ᕫO ᕫEAVEN

The storm-rainbow scenario is what keeps me looking to the east. Some day, the clouds will part and this same Jesus who has bragging rights over sin and death will appear and there will be no need to capture it on camera because He will have captured me.

*At once I was in the Spirit, and there before me was a throne in heaven with someone sitting on it. And the one who sat there had the appearance of jasper and ruby. A rainbow that shone like an emerald encircled the throne.*

**Revelation 4:2 (NIV)**

May
PORTALS
To HEAVEN

But I thought...

There were twenty-five of us at the reunion...

We were former members of a "retired church" where some were so passionate about what God was doing that they lived together in a large retreat house and in other homes spread across thirty-nine acres. The big mansion and the peaceful property became symbols of community and unity for the region's greater church body. Thousands had visited and others moved from far and wide to be part of this community.

Movements experience ebbs and flows and there were moments when the slower times brought forth prophecies that "the latter glory of this 'house' would be greater than the former one" - a quote from Haggai 2:9.

There were many surges and it appeared that the prophecy was about to come true only to have another ebb overcome that flow. Even as the literal doors were closing at our beloved community, many other doors would soon swing wide open. Former members filled leadership roles in other churches and mission organizations while other became marketplace witnesses.

## PORTAL TO HEAVEN

At the reunion, our former pastor's wife keenly observed:"I was always disappointed that the Haggai prophecy never came about. But seeing all of you here who are serving and being sent in so many ways, I realize that 'we' are that 'house.'"This should make everyone feel better when God doesn't follow our script.

*'For My thoughts are not your thoughts, Nor are your ways My ways,' declares The Lord.*

**Isaiah 55:8 (NASB), Also read: Matthew 1:23 (KJV)**

But I thought...

When I was five, I had a nightmare that I was holding my mom's hand one minute and in the next I was confronting a big robot on my own. Losing mom's hand was the unthinkable. I woke up in a sweat. It's one of the few childhood dreams that I can remember...

One of the more defining moments of unspoken expectation in my life occurred when the unexpected visited my family. My sister explained to me that my mother's formerly-diagnosed sciatica was actually a large intestinal tumor. It was so shocking that it would take years before I realized that in some naïve way, I had certain plans for life that God was not supposed to monkey with.

Four months after that diagnosis, the heart of our home stopped beating. Two years later, my dad joined her and the rug of my life had been pulled out from under me.

Although we were all younger adults at this point, we were suddenly the older generation. Holiday meals felt like we were sipping make-believe tea in tiny plastic cups at the kiddy table.

## PORTAL TO HEAVEN

I lost my mother's hand in the dream and later in life. Yet, Mom and Dad's legacy didn't depart when they did. Our family still holds tight to the hand that gave us our parent's hands, faith and values.

*For I am the LORD your God, the one who takes hold of your right hand, who says to you, 'Don't be afraid, I am helping you.'*

**Isaiah 41:13 (NET)**
**Also read: Psalm 61:2 25:4 (NASB), Psalm 23:1,4b,6a (ESV)**

"In this world nothing can be said to be certain, except death and taxes."

After all the military, political, familial, emotional and psychological upheaval of The American Revolution, it's understandable that Benjamin Franklin would feel this way.

But Ole' Ben left out another certainty: change. Living through that war and the break with Great Britain and all of the positioning that was taking place, one would think Franklin would have included change as the new normal.

You don't have to be part of a revolution to figure out that everything you bank on will probably disappear in the next few years, decades or half-century. And with the throttling up of the information age and the instant tweet, text or simulcast, there is almost a disappearance of consistency.

It would be difficult to completely disengage in an effort to protect ourselves from the emotional overload and the rapidity of change that also seems to be crowding out one-to-one relationships that used to be the basis for consistency.

## PORTAL TO HEAVEN

God has placed needs right in front of us in order that we become the positive change in the lives of others. Change isn't all bad. A wound that's treated changes from grotesque to invisible and that's a good thing. A pat on the back can change a day. And so on and so forth. Ben Franklin was close except for one thing. He left out Jesus who was taxed for our debt but is still alive. Jesus' permanency changes everything.

*'I am the Alpha and the Omega,' says the Lord God, 'who is, and who was, and who is to come, the Almighty.'*

**Revelation 1:8 (NIV), Also read: John 8:58 (NIV), Acts 17:28 (NIV)**

Have you ever noticed that God's sense of direction is perfect? Is this why the term "GPS" stands for "God's Positioning System?"

When I was very young and even more naïve, I lost my way. I then lost my job in public relations and felt led to assist non-profits as a consultant in that same field. The only trouble was that non-profits didn't have any profits left over for me. This unmitigated financial disaster caused problems at home and jaded my thinking about service to God.

I was lost. "But I thought if I gave everything over to You that You would take care of me," I told God.

In His grace, a job came that led to a career that changed my life. Interestingly, that young self of mine murmured all along the way to the prosperity and freedom that God was bringing to me. One wise teacher noted that "disillusionment" like mine is simply the discovery of an illusion.

This idea of God taking us in a different direction than we expected is actually part of the process of getting to know Him. After all was said and done, I found that my original desires were simply met in a different way than I expected.

## ᴘORTAL ᴛO ʜEAVEN

Recognize the motivation behind God's leading. Then, when God seems to be getting lost or going out of the way of our GPS, we are in a better position to enjoy the scenery.

*When I left home and crossed the Jordan River, I owned nothing except a walking stick. Now my household fills two large camps...The sun was rising as Jacob left Peniel and he was limping because of the injury to his hip.*

**"Jacob's Journey" as recorded in Genesis 32:10, 31 (NLT)**

Expectation is a dangerous thing.

On the one hand, we must have desires because they fuel everything. On the other, we must be careful that our desires line up with God's will. That's where the trouble lies.

We can even use scripture to gift-wrap our desires. The early followers thought they found a present in Jesus Christ. Therefore, we are in good company!

They thought they recognized a deliverer when they saw one. After all, it was the perfect set-up. No one talked with such authority. No one else had ever performed such miracles.

Even Peter was sure of what God had in store for, well, God.

Not so fast. *"Jesus, knowing that they intended to come and make him king by force, withdrew again to a mountain by himself."* (John 6:15, NIV) Even the last question asked of Jesus proved that they were still hunting for a good candidate for the primaries: "Then they gathered around him and asked him, *'Lord, are you at this time going to restore the kingdom to Israel?'"* (Acts 1:6, NIV)

## PORTAL TO HEAVEN

The "But-I-thought-syndrome" has been around for thousands of years and we suffer from it individually and corporately. Next time we get the idea that we are sure we know exactly what God is up to, we should take a "chill pill" and gift-wrap our desires in this scripture:

*So here's what I want you to do, God helping you: Take your everyday, ordinary life—your sleeping, eating, going-to-work, and walking-around life—and place it before God as an offering.*

**Romans 12:1 (The Message)**

There were no malls when I was a child.

"Back to school" meant back to the "dry goods" store.

This is where the basics sat piled on tables. White underwear, white t-shirts and fairly simple shirts (not white, whew) were the order of the day. When a woman has seven children, white is good.

Cheap is even better because all kids start their school at the same time of year.

We came across some sweaters. They were not on her white sheet of paper that listed Mom's black-and-white priorities. But sweaters come in handy in The Fall in New Jersey. At thirteen, I was clueless that they were budget-busters. But my admiration for one did not escape her notice. She insisted that I try it on. I could tell it pleased her as much as it did me.

That sweater joined all of the whites in the bag – including that white register sales slip that was just a little bit longer than she expected. But moms understand their children's desires even when they are a shade off.

## PORTAL TO HEAVEN

Kids grow into more than sweaters by watching our moms. Mom passed on many years ago. I still put that sweater on at least once a year. She'd be pleased to know that even more than the sweater, its lesson keeps me warm.

*...do not forsake your mother's teaching; Indeed, they are a graceful wreath to your head and ornaments about your neck.*

**Proverbs 1:8,9 (NASB)**

Mother's Day carries so many themes in its attempt to define the essence of the divine-designed feminine heart and particularly its role in bringing forth life – literally and figuratively. While Mom birthed us, we must grow to learn how Mom can be reproduced in us.

The feminine heart flourishes like the colors, flowers and scents of the month it is celebrated in. It's only right that Mother's Day falls in the heart of the tenderness of May – the month that represents seasonal compassion in so many climates.

The example that mothers put forth are as much for males as for females. Could you imagine a school, college, business, or government run by anyone who had not been influenced by his or her mom? Life would be like a boot camp.

## PORTAL TO HEAVEN

Mothers are the metaphor for understanding how God brings forth life. Whether that life is in the form of a dream or service or career or in the natural desire to reproduce her ways in the form of starting our own families, mom is a direct representation of He who is the life and the light of men.

*In him was life, and that life was the light of all mankind.*

**John 1:4 (NIV)**

Whether an offspring is male or female, that child should be enlarged by the one who carried him or her.

This theme of being carried takes us in one direction: up. Think on how our spirits were birthed in the heart of heaven. Who carried us from concept to reality?

Mother's Day helps us paint a picture of the aspirations of the divine. Every mother rubs her belly as the baby grows. She will take care of herself. She will talk to the embryo. She will sing to the little one. She will wonder. She will carry them through cold, heat and even illnesses. She will worry. She may do any number of things.

This assignment of carrying is only given to one person in our lives.

## PORTAL TO HEAVEN

Mother's Day is a bonanza for the greeting card industry. You don't even have to employ a poet there. You just need to hire a thankful son or daughter and that alone will carry the day.

*He took with him Mary, to whom he was engaged, who was now expecting a child. And while they were there, the time came for her baby to be born. She gave birth to her firstborn son.*

**Luke 2:5-7 (NLT)**

I read my daughter's mind…

Waiting for a waitress seems like an oxymoron. Yet every mom with young and fidgety kids knows this scene all too well. They have ants in their pants and it seems like they were born to embarrass Mom in front of the entire restaurant through the utter display of her inability to control them in even the slightest manner.

"Quick," my daughter thinks, "I've got to grab the waitress' attention and get some crayons." Sure enough, she flags down the familiar server and before long her kids are a bit more docile once they settle in to drawing on the back of the paper placemat.

When my daughter was a child, Mom would instruct her and her sister through "Art 201" – art for two's and ones. That same manner now keeps them busy at this restaurant and they actually come out with some fine placemat masterpieces.

My wife has gotten in on the act since they were toddlers and has an entire cabinet filled with all sorts of rainy-day drawing books and exercises.

## PORTAL TO HEAVEN

Art exhibits just one way that the intergenerational blessings of mothers portray the patience and guidance of God. Picture that.

*[I am filled with] joy, when I call to remembrance the genuine faith that is in you, which dwelt first in your grandmother Lois and your mother Eunice, and I am persuaded is in you also.*

**2 Timothy 1:5 (NKJV). Editor's brackets.**

"That's because you're not a mother," was my wife's quick and nonchalant reply. It was a simple enough conversation about our kids. As usual on that topic, she was right. Only mothers can really understand...

I have had the privilege of knowing moms of all types. None of them are perfect and none of them have raised pain-free kids. But the one thing I know about mothers is that they probably have the deepest understanding of the child's idiosyncratic mannerisms and nuances.

My mother-figure raised her kids during the unruly 1960's. With horror and fear, she visited her rebellious daughter in a hippie commune where drugs were aplenty and her son-in-law had gone off to the Far East to study mysticism.

Another friend walked alongside her son despite his alcoholism and loved him every drink of the way while she learned the differences between enabling and tough love.

Still another mother I know well lost more sleep in sixteen years than most would in two lifetimes as she cared for and cried over her boy with cystic fibrosis all the way to his teenage passing. Even now, she still holds him in her heart.

In my involvement with the inner city, I have witnessed the broken heart of mothers whose sons and daughters have landed in jail – and this too common a tragedy at that.

## PORTAL TO HEAVEN

The relentless love of a mother is a takes us straight into the heart of God so that all of us who are not mothers will "get it."

*The faithful love of the LORD never ends! His mercies never cease.*

**Lamentations 3:22 (NLT)**

Deliberately looking for pride in our life is a good habit – especially when it's disguised so superbly.

"I think he struggles with pride," I say, not realizing that I just exhibited that very sin.

However, if pride-detecting is taken to an obsession, the utter thrill of this grand and noble hobby might put us on an obnoxious path to false humility – the "worst kind of pride" if there is such a thing.

But a healthy awareness of my pride is a good thing. Once my radar picks up and shoots down pride in any one area, I have to be careful not be prideful about my humility.

There's a fine line between enjoying our talents because they are gifts from God and slipping into a prideful ownership of those same abilities. A powerful exertion of this principle is to be found in the movie, "Chariots of Fire." Olympic medalist and missionary Eric Liddell allays his sister's worry that his competing is based in pride. "God made me fast. And when I run, I feel His pleasure," Liddell explains. "To give it up would be to hold Him in contempt - to win is to honor Him."

Arriving at that kind of conclusion is true freedom and victory in this race-to-the-finish against pride.

## PORTAL TO HEAVEN

Imagine a metal detector that God turns into a pride detector for our hearts. While we may feel crushed by what His detector finds, we will not be crushed by a God who honors our desires to be discovered.

*Search me, O God, and know my heart: try me, and know my thoughts…*

**Psalm 139:23 (ESV)**

When I was "yung 'n dumb," I got excited about the idea of serving in God's kingdom in a way that only I had insight enough to figure out.

I had the brilliant concept of starting a consultant business for ministries that didn't understand the benefits of promotion, networking and organizational growth. While I should have known better about the realities of finances because I had been married and had one child at that point, I somehow had enough pride that overshadowed any sense of pragmatism.

I was the messiah of public relations. People –and non-profits and ministries – will always welcome a "free messiah." (Translation: To their enjoyment, I worked for very little pay.) I multiplied their loaves while not putting any bread on mine.

Working nights and leaving my wife and child home alone while trying to peck out a living during the day with my important ministry led to horrific personal and financial consequences. If there had been a "Pride-Hunter" gizmo on the market at that time, some of my friends and church leaders would have all come to my birthday party with the same gift.

## PORTAL TO HEAVEN

Pride is awfully hard to search out and so God will multiply these lessons in our lives just as he did with the loaves. Repeatedly biting into bread might not be as tasty as humble pie, but if bread is slang for cash, it can be just as effective.

*The heart is deceitful above all things, and desperately wicked; who can know it? I, the Lord, search the heart, I test the mind, even to give every man according to his ways, according to the fruit [bread] of his doings.*

**Jeremiah 17:9,10 (NKJV)**

I remember talking with my cousin when we were just youngsters. We began talking about sports. It began with him encouraging me about my athletic abilities. Somehow, I thought he wasn't so good at running, but said he "wasn't that bad." That inflamed his nine-year-old ego and he immediately challenged me to a race in the front yard. The sad ending to that story was that I was beaten pretty badly.

Humility is the teacher that sounds like she's repeating herself. Evaluating myself in each of our thousands of situations is hard. I'm not alone. This race scenario was repeated several years later with a cocky high school classmate who was our ace third baseman. To his shock, I whipped him in a barefoot dash on the beach. It doesn't stop with us little people.

A world-renown boxer may brag before big fights. But when he is on his back in the fourth round and the cameras are flashing and his opponent is gleefully raising his hands and prancing around him and he can't seem to get off the canvas, he has found that he misjudged his abilities and didn't exactly have a perfect perception of reality.

## PORTAL TO HEAVEN

God doesn't look at us as better or less than the next person. In some pure fatherly, non-favoring way that is hard for us to both imagine and accept and results in us repeatedly feeling the need to compete, He loves us the way we are – even when He is helping us off the canvas.

*Look beneath the surface so you can judge correctly...Do not think of yourself more highly than you ought, but rather think of yourself with sober judgment... sin is crouching at your door; it desires to have you, but you must rule over it.*

**John 7:24 (NLT), Romans 12:3 (NIV), Genesis 4:7 (NIV)**

"How cheesy is that?" "No one would have said that!" "Everyone knows everyone. What a coincidence." "There's not one African American or Latino in the movie." "The same guy who starred in this film also wrote it, produced it and I think his name appeared in the credits as part of the catering service." "Did you notice how everything worked out so perfectly in the end and they all come to know Jesus?"

No, I wasn't a Christian movie critic. I was a prideful Christian.

As a writer, I knew that movie projects could take a dozen years from conception to distribution. Yet, these independent filmmakers were doing this on a shoestring budget and that meant casting volunteer actors and using screenwriters who were just cutting their teeth. So, while I appreciated their guts, it was their art that made me choke on my popcorn.

Then, I tried it myself. I was passionate about my projects and had great screenplays with hot subject matter. That's when I bumped into some of the harsh realities of moviemaking. For finances, I tried crowd-funding and networking with interest-groups. For production, I spoke with filmmakers. And on and on. I was viewed as a pest at best or a competitor at worst. Everyone had their own project.

A few years later, I was back in the theaters with a greater appreciation for independent filmmakers.

## PORTAL TO HEAVEN

Pride has a way of writing bad scripts for our lives.

*Do not think of yourself more highly than you ought, but rather think of yourself with sober judgment…*

**Romans 12:3 (NIV)**

Many have come to the conclusion that the Second Coming of Jesus Christ is imminent. They point to the statehood of Israel and many apocalyptic signs. Moreover, technology could exponentially make The Great Commission a completed task.

Some theorize that the only thing stopping the return of Jesus is pagans and politicians. Atheism produces pagan politicians who keep their citizens dependent upon them for jobs, finances and food. In short, these pagan nations stand in the way of the gospel. What's a missionary to do?

Actually, the secret to the return of Christ is spelled out in The Gospel of John in Chapter 17. Here, Jesus lays out a plan for the church individually and corporately: Get along.

There's only one thing in the way: pride. The very same thing that caused the need for Jesus to come in the first place is the exact thing that prevents Him coming a second time.

Harry Truman said that anything could be accomplished if everyone agreed that no one person should get the credit. If Truman had added that all honor must go to Christ, he would have nailed it. Jesus will return when His church is one as the Father and He are one.

## PORTAL TO HEAVEN

Jesus assigned our unity as the forerunner for The King's coming. Pagans and politicians are pushovers compared with pride. May the glory of Christ be our only aim. The rest will take care of itself.

*For jealousy and selfishness are not God's kind of wisdom. Such things are earthly, unspiritual, and demonic.*

**James 3:15 (NLT)**
**Also read: 2 Samuel 18:18 (NIV), 1 Samuel 15:12 (NIV)**

Memorial Day should make us squirm as we remember the dead soldiers this day honors. The irony of this holiday is that millions of Americans forget.

While it is natural to want to take advantage of a long weekend and hit the beach, we may do well to remember those who hit the beach and never returned. That isn't a pleasant thought and it's even more disturbing when we picture the profile of those who gave it all.

Often, they were young men at the height of their physical selves. One old vet soberly related his experience. "I was eighteen," he said. And then he went on about getting past his "first kill." After that, "you don't think about it." Furthermore, he made it clear that he is not interested in military reunions or anything that brings up memories of that time.

He made it back.

But what if a fallen hero could return and go through the details of how he was eliminated?

Memorial Day was established to bring us closer to the reality of sacrifice and help us cling to memories we'd rather forget. To put it bluntly, it's a long way from the pleasures of a barbeque.

## PORTAL TO HEAVEN

If Memorial Day makes us remember what we'd conveniently forget, it has served its purpose.

*Greater love has no one than this: to lay down one's life for one's friends.*

**John 15:13 (NIV)**

Special operations troops or pilots pinned down behind enemy lines in Vietnam were always glad to have the Jolly Green Giant nearby. No, they weren't snacking on frozen peas in the swamps and jungles of Laos. This search and rescue helicopter was nicknamed after that friendly fellow on the vegetable commercials because of its green shades and its large size.

The whirlybird was known for many features including its ability to go long distances. But its protective armor allowed it hover in the middle of hostile fire, allowing enough time to get the soldiers on board and get the heck out of there.

Engineers and military strategists had to think long and hard to come up with well-equipped flying machines that would do a job based around specific needs (i.e. downed pilots, jungles, challenging terrain).

Base commanders put paratroopers through some of the highest-attrition two-year training programs in order to man these rescue team helicopters.

It took years of brilliant design work, strategizing, training and brave execution to save even one pilot or special ops troop trapped in the hellish jungles of enemy territory.

## PORTAL TO HEAVEN

God put the full weight of heaven's resources behind His search and rescue for our souls.

*I have not come on my own; God sent me…For God so loved the world that he gave his one and only Son, that whoever believes in him shall not perish but have eternal life…So if the Son sets you free, you will be free indeed.*

**John 8: 42b (NIV), John 3:16 (NIV), John 8:36 (NIV)**

Obviously, military tactics are worse than a game of chess. Yet, that kind of strategy is exactly what leaders must employ.

The only difference is that making a wrong move in a battle may cost your life and the ones of those around you.

Extending the chess analogy, I give up my castle for your queen. Baiting an enemy into a trap is one of the sneakiest and oldest traps in war.

In biblical times, the Israelites on at least two occasions drew enemies away from cities with faux retreats. When the enemy left their town to chase the Israelites, a hidden wing of their army would capture or destroy the undefended city.

More recently, the North Vietnamese baited American forces by allowing surrounded U.S. troops to live long enough to call for reinforcements in the form of helicopters. In essence, they were using the pinned-down troops to sucker helicopters that were the real prize. Then, they'd shoot down the multi-million dollar helicopters. Downed choppers made great American television footage - inflaming the anti-war protests back on U.S. soil.

## PORTAL TO HEAVEN

We often get drawn into traps even when we are trying to spiritually advance. Our walk with God and others is not just a friendly chess match and sucker punches is what our enemy specializes in.

*Be alert and of sober mind. Your enemy the devil prowls around like a roaring lion looking for someone to devour...For our struggle is not against flesh and blood, but against the rulers, against the authorities, against the powers of this dark world and against the spiritual forces of evil in the heavenly realm.*

**1 Peter 5:8 (NIV), Ephesians 6:12 (NIV)**

The dark Vietnamese jungle creeps with unfriendly possibilities for the downed, dehydrated American pilot with the broken leg limping behind enemy lines. He wonders just how many steps away his would-be captors are...

"Will my team come for me?" "How will they find me in this hellhole?" "Will the North Vietnamese get me first?"

Even though the military spares no expense and risk lives in various helicopter rescue attempts, the time leading up to those efforts seems like an eternity as he waits and waits. Doubt drains him even though he knows well the determination and courage of his comrades. His vulnerability is heightened by an overwhelming sense of loneliness.

Beyond the loyalty of his friends, the equipment used in these operations is second to none.

The dangling rope that all his hopes literally and figuratively hang onto has a steel core and strands and strands tested to ratings beyond the imagination. For the manufacturers of such lifelines, there is no such thing as "overkill."

One rescuer was dropped to hold a pilot. As the two are hoisted aboard, the rescued pilot's repeated thought was, "Please don't let go of me...Please don't let go of me...Please don't let me go." Even after all it took for his buddies to save him, the pilot was still worried about being dropped.

## PORTAL TO HEAVEN

Our experience tells us that Jesus has saved us through everything. Like the pilot, we cry, "Don't let go of me!" We think this is his first ropin' rodeo.

*...[He] gave Himself for our sins to rescue us from the present evil age...*

**Galatians 1:4 (BSB). Editor's brackets.**

The roar of the helicopter is all you know. Suddenly, it touches down and you are in an open field on the edge of a Laos jungle. When the chopper lifts off and disappears, it is eerily quiet. As you approach the tree line, you hear nothing but the wind and some monkeys, insects and birds…

One special operations soldier was impressed with the need to listen to the animal kingdom so he would recognize changes in those sounds. If a sudden disruption to vocal patterns occurred, it could mean that unseen enemy soldiers were moving or planning a surprise attack.

Mary Beth Metzger, who has been blind for sixty years, sums it up: "You develop a sense of what's important," she said. "You can't listen too hard to only on one thing. You must pay attention to the overall sounds. In a new environment, you have to focus very sharply. When I come to a crosswalk, my life is on the line and I must trust my hearing."

The soldiers dropped off behind enemy lines have a mission that 99.99999% of the rest of the military do not have. They also have training that most do not. Their job is to gather intelligence. One soldier said that 200 of these men essentially kept 40,000-60,000 North Vietnamese off the South Vietnamese fronts - a heck of a ratio. Who could estimate how many troops they saved as a result of their sacrifice?

## PORTAL TO HEAVEN

God assigns unique jobs that may require that we see with our ears. Who knows how many souls will be saved through our faith and obedience?

*…obey the LORD your God and carefully follow all his commands I give you today… See, I have given you this land. Go in and take possession…Jesus answered, 'If I want him to remain alive until I return, what is that to you? You must follow me.'*

**Deuteronomy 28:1, Deuteronomy 1:8, John 21:22 (All NIV)**

Exiting the interstate, I notice a highway drainage pond in the middle of the cloverleaf. The ducks there were mostly oblivious to the traffic and noise.

It had become their home, a habitat of polluted convenience.

"Let's get away from this incessant noise before our ducklings are choked by the exhaust or, worse yet, are killed by all of this speeding traffic," Mama Duck says to her hubby. "This is no place for our kiddies."

Hubby either doesn't step up or becomes comfortable.

## PORTAL TO HEAVEN

There is a similarity of our habitat, the earth, and that dirty pond. One wonders how much crud has slowly attached to us. After 6,000 years, is it possible that we are not noticing anymore?

*Pure and undefiled religion in the sight of our God and Father is this: to visit orphans and widows in their distress, and to keep oneself unstained by the world.*

**James 1:27 (NASB)**

Was Eden in Jersey?

The ducks quacking in the interstate cloverleaf pond remind me of The Garden State, the "What Exit State," or as it is most commonly referenced," New Joisey."

The "What Exit" reputation was only exacerbated by Simon and Garfunkle's famous line: "…counting the cars on The New Jersey Turnpike, they're all going to look for America."

Perhaps they found it in New York or Philadelphia - barely noticing our gardens on the way.

On top of all of that, New Jersey did have some pollution concerns. To that point, traveling into Manhattan takes you over what Simon and Garfunkle might refer to as "bridges over troubled waters." Darkened and accented with floating metal scraps and old tires, these brooks and rivers were the waterways where the Lenni-Lenape Indians looked for America and found it in their catch of the day.

## PORTAL TO HEAVEN

Many Jersey-ites have to go away to find themselves. The polluted, crowded and noisy state of my hometown state shows just how far we have canoed from Eden. Would I trade the advances in medicine, technology and transportation for Eden? If the oily ducks in the middle of that cloverleaf pond could talk, they might call us a bunch of quacks.

*Now the LORD God had planted a garden in the east, in Eden; and there he put the man he had formed. The LORD God made all kinds of trees grow out of the ground–trees that were pleasing to the eye and good for food. In the middle of the garden were the tree of life and the tree of the knowledge of good and evil. A river watering the garden flowed from Eden; from there it was separated into four headwaters.*

**Genesis 2:8-10 (NIV)**

Lord Tennyson, Walt Whitman, John Keats, Samuel Taylor Coleridge, Elizabeth Barrett Browning, William Blake, Emily Dickinson, Robert Frost and William Butler Yeats were all poets whose pens were inspired by birds.

In our area, birds are the most persistent alarm clocks of May. They are my first awareness that my dreams are no longer my reality.

Having been in the hearing aid field for many years, I have heard story after story about birds.

"I walked out to the parking lot with my new hearing aids," one patient told me, "and I couldn't figure out what all the noise was about. Then, I suddenly realized I was hearing birds for the first time in over twenty years."

Even absent of hearing difficulties, I don't notice the birds as prominently as summer approaches because I begin to take them for granted. And yet, they continue to sing some of the same sonnets that they tweeted to the greatest poets.

## PORTAL TO HEAVEN

Our indifference is like the distance between Eden and us. Time brings us further away from the songs that these creatures must have sung in that unblemished garden. Oh, but there is a man who sings a song taught by his father and it leads me back to heaven on earth for now and then someday forever.

*'No one ever spoke the way this man does,' the guards replied...And they sang a new song before the throne and before the four living creatures and the elders."*

**John 7:46 (NIV), Revelation 14:3 (NIV)**

I took a walk with my beloved just before sunset on a road surrounded by woods.

The persistence and volume of the birds sounded like a jungle when an intruder walks around unannounced. Perhaps they were tucking their little ones in and what I was hearing were either the baby birdies fussing before or after their collective nighty-night prayers. I chose to believe the latter.

If those chirps were near my bedroom window, I would not have been able to go to sleep myself no matter how many evening prayers I said. And I always thought these creatures were loudest in the morning.

Birds step it up for our sakes at night. Might they somehow know that long days wear us down? Their songs remind us of heaven's symphonies and choirs just when we need it.

It is so easy to slip away from the wonders of God in our weariness that He makes us stumble over Eden's memories.

Some have said that the stains and strains of the day require an evening spiritual bath in the form of bible reading and prayer. I have noticed that I am vulnerable to negativity and discouragement when I am tired and that is a temptation that no mortal can afford.

## PORTAL TO HEAVEN

If God chooses jungle-like decibels to wake me up before tucking me in, I shall not argue with the teller of the bedtime stories of Eden.

*...we do not have a high priest who is unable to sympathize with our weaknesses, but one who in every respect has been tempted as we are, yet without sin... For he knows how weak we are; he remembers we are only dust.*

**Heb. 4:15 (ESV), Ps. 103:14 (NLT)**

It's an entrancing, dancing May morning.

The sun hired The Hudson River to add a false front of fog. Barely hiding behind the waterway, that fiery ball has begun to spread its wings to take us into the flight of a new day.

I step out onto the porch and the turkeys shoo every which way as if I'm a hired assassin in November. I can clearly hear the pecking of the more reliable and less skittish starlings beneath the bird feeder. A chipmunk climbs the rhododendron within arms reach as a blue jay flies by and a squirrel scurries to get in on the action near the feeder. It's a veritable town square! Our cats are content to watch the show. I pull up a seat as well.

Why would we trade Our Father's estate with its verdant voice for the call of the swine's squeal?

The Prodigal Son of today feeds on the scraps of pornography, adultery, gambling, drugs, alcohol, etc. We claim it will never happen to us. Then how do we explain the proclivity of even people of faith to make all of this so popular? Vice has so many de-vices. If it's not alcohol, it that "one thing." And so it goes until each of us has at least a splatter of the pig's muck on our fashionable fig leaves.

## ᏢORTAL ᏩᎢᴏ ᎻEAVEN

The Town Square is the portal to heaven because it's a place to gather with those who know a pigpen from a bird feeder.

*We all, like sheep, have gone astray, each of us has turned to our own way; and the LORD has laid on him the iniquity of us all... When he came to his senses, he said... 'I will set out and go back to my father and say to him: Father, I have sinned against heaven and against you.'*

**Isaiah 53:6 (NIV), Luke 15:17ff (NIV)**

# PEN YOUR PORTALS

June
PORTALS
To HEAVEN

Wandering mesmerized through the famed Rose Garden in Portland, Oregon, is probably a common occurrence. Shutterbugs from around the world snap 'n' sniff. It's nothing short of euphoric. And if the beauty of the roses isn't enough, the design and layout of the gardens are an entrancing portal into a fifth dimension of beauty that I have never visited.

I turned right. Panoramic. I looked down. Close-up. I walked under an arch. Click. I looked at my daughter's eyes. "Would you mind taking one of my daughter and me?" One of the plethora of photographers was pleased to provide us with a pic...

We were all here for the same reason: to witness the stunning, but narrow, window of this extraterrestrial beauty.

But wait! The gardener is carrying a huge clear plastic bag of dead rose pedals. I'm as crushed as some of these petals under my foot. The sacred lies in a see-through tomb.

Strong young men and beautiful girls would hardly understand the metaphor before me. But the brevity of beauty and strength is something we should all contemplate.

Take all the pictures you want. Enjoy the fragrances of every good thing God gives you on this earth. But you're not being a killjoy if you happen to notice a few dead petals and a gardener who can barely keep up. You're being observant.

## PORTAL TO HEAVEN

Thinking metaphorically, dead petals could influence what we plant in our gardens.

*Don't let the excitement of youth cause you to forget your Creator. Honor him in your youth before you grow old...*

**Ecclesiastes 12:1 (NLT)**

"I'm the cutest kid in the class," I declared to my eighth grade nun who gave me "the eye"...

Most remember a much bigger boast. While many insist that John Lennon's quote about being more popular than Jesus Christ was taken out of context, it's easy to figure out that there was something in his heart that slipped through his lips.

"I'm the greatest" was Muhammad Ali's tagline and his boasting was a matter of habit. Well before he died, life had him on the ropes after throwing him some punches. He probably wished he could throw out his boastings.

There was an ancient, broken statue of a ruler that was discovered in the middle of a dessert. After it was uncovered and cleaned up, the pitiful epitaph gloated about being the greatest monarch in history. To this day, no one knows who the guy was.

The greatest written treasury of famous people only gives the most noted a paragraph or two.

## PORTAL TO HEAVEN

We must be circumspect about our position or station in life because it is so fleeting and it is given by God as a gift. We mustn't violate the code of Christ "who being in very nature God did not consider it robbery but made Himself of no reputation." (Philippians 2:6,7) Of course, the paradox here in the upside down kingdom of God is that His humility ends up exalting Him to the highest place.

*For by the grace given me I say to every one of you: Do not think of yourself more highly than you ought, but rather think of yourself with sober judgment, in accordance with the faith God has distributed to each of you.*

**Romans 12:3 (NIV)**

Political campaigns are launched, by nature, through a boast.

In the case of American presidential elections, each candidate who has ever run has to deliver a Messianic message in order to make it into the primaries. Beginning with their home state, they must establish their message, garner a following, recruit some friends with a little extra cash and repeat the following over and over and over again: "The last guy was terrible. I am going to do better. I am going to change Washington, D.C."This is the specific boast.

In most cases, their backstory better be good: "I cut taxes, grew businesses, working men and poor got a fair shake and the world is a safer place under my leadership," they claim.

When they finally get elected, they find that Washington, D.C. has more gridlocks than Manhattan traffic from the disparity that the founding fathers intentionally established. You can't speed during rush hour in New York City.

When they become a lame duck and most of their campaign boasts sound hollow, the average Joe watching television exclaims, "Look how gray his hair is and how he has aged."

They found out what that last guy knew – but only a long time after they were placed their hand on The Bible.

## PORTAL TO HEAVEN

Godly leadership will always come in the form of servanthood. Heaven came to serve. Humanity has been boasting about Jesus ever since and His kingdom reigns forever. We find that out when we place our hand on The Bible…and then open it up.

*Though he was God, he did not think of equality with God as something to cling to… he gave up his divine privileges; he took the humble position of a slave… He will reign over the house of Jacob forever, and His kingdom will have no end."*

**Ph. 2:6,7, (NLT), Luke 1:33 (NASB)**

He was tall. He was handsome. He was successful. He was polite. He lived in a beautiful colonial in a historic neighborhood. His wife was lovely.

Many years later, he tracked me down for some help with his hearing. He was now living in an assisted living facility. The adult home was the kind with Grandfather clocks, cherry-wood libraries, heated swimming pools and the most attentive staff anyone could want.

He was now walking with a cane and an irregular shuffle, leaning to the right a lot, especially before seating himself in his automatic-elevating lounge chair.

He wasn't as tall because of that bent-condition. He had lost some hair. He obviously still had some cash or he couldn't have afforded luxury housing. But compared to his former colonial, this apartment looked like nothing more than a comfortable exile-cell.

His world had shrunk. He was removed from the influence he once had back in his hometown.

The setting and person may change, but aging has a 100% track record.

## PORTAL TO HEAVEN

All of the props will eventually be removed from our lives. Viewing life from this perspective doesn't have to make us depressed. But there would be nothing wrong if it would make us more humble.

*As for the days of our life, they contain seventy years, Or if due to strength, eighty years, Yet their pride is but labor and sorrow; For soon it is gone and we fly away.*

**Psalm 90:10 (NASB)**

There is a chance that you will outlive someone sitting near you or who is living or working with you. It could be a spouse. It could be a friend. Siblings don't live forever. Perhaps it's your neighbor. Certain classmates are going to be missing at reunions. These thoughts don't have to be morbid. In fact, they can be life-giving.

When we understand the brevity of relationships and of life itself, we tend to look into the eyes of others through different eyes.

It can change everything. Being caught up in "the now" can sometimes make circumstances large and relationships small.

When we begin to see the finish line, we will tend to think of strategies that will help that loved one make it to the end. That changes "the now" into a part of an overall and purposeful journey.

Jesus is the master of the delicate balance of understanding "the now" and "the destination." In each of the moments where he stops to speak with someone, he is compassionate within that moment. But he is also using the present to take them into their future.

When it came to himself, he was always steadily moving toward the cross. His eyes were fixed on eternity without losing "the now."

## PORTAL TO HEAVEN

Think on eternity and help others and you walk in that manner in "the now" and all thoughts that this is morbid will be dead.

*LORD, make me to know my end and what is the extent of my days; let me know how transient I am… Jesus stopped…*

**Psalm 39:4 (NASB), Luke 18:40 (NIV)**

"Good, Good Father" is a popular worship song that will probably be included in many church's playlist on Father's Day from now until the end of time. Its repetitive nature underscores God's very nature.

But many have asked, "What kind of God would allow ___?"

God's apparent distance seems to be at the bottom of the inferred question, "Is God really good?"

A good father raises a child to maturity by allowing them to fall off bikes, go through unnecessary break-ups and find that friendships have a betrayal side. But a good father is also always within reach with counsel so that foolishness doesn't have to be inevitable and self-inflicted wounds don't have to lead to years of dysfunction and elongated pity parties. He also understands the pain of a son when life hands out unfair sentences.

For Christians, God has given us the scriptures. When studied and applied through The Holy Spirit, they lead us just as if Our Father was right alongside us. He also gave His Son as the perfect example of how to live through circumstance when life doesn't make sense and disappointments and inequities begin to look like skyscrapers.

## ᏢORTAL ᏫO ᎻEAVEN

Every day is Father's Day in his kingdom. We would all do well to consider the obvious evidences of His goodness and perhaps find out that there's good reason for the repetition in "Good, Good Father."

*I will not leave you as orphans [comfortless, bereaved, and helpless]; I will come [back] to you....No one is good–except God alone...The Holy Spirit is coming. He will lead you into all truth.*

**John 14:18 (AMP), Mark 10:18b (NIV), John 16:13 (NLV)**

Having lost my father in my twenties, I have discovered that my memories of him are getting more distant with age. But there are a couple of pearls of wisdom that I keep in the vault of my heart.

Dad was a plumber. We (or should I say "He") were working on a project when he gave me this advice: "Always keep one hand free. You can't do two things at once." Or something like that. As I said, it's been a long time.

That may not sound profound. To me, it was utterly prophetic.

I am a self-diagnosed A.D.D.-meister. I never do one thing at a time. I've been known to climb three sets of stairs three times, only to finally remember why I went up and down the previous two times. Once, I was writing three songs at one time while precariously driving. (I probably misplaced them. Oh, well.)

Sooooo, I go into the Pearls-of-Wisdom Safe (if I can remember the combination), and pull out Dad's advice whenever I literally or figuratively have too many things in my hands at once. What's better yet, his advice works.

## PORTAL TO HEAVEN

God gave me the dad I needed.
Even though I lost him and some of his advice, I've found that the best gift a dad can receive on Father's Day and everyday is having his kids listen to him.

*Listen, my sons, to a father's instruction; pay attention and gain understanding. I give you sound learning, so do not forsake my teaching…Take hold of my words with all your heart; keep my commands, and you will live.*

**Proverbs 4:1-4 (NIV)**

When I think of the brilliance of Einstein and the details and trials of Edison, I get a little intimidated.

My trouble is that I was born with a simple brain. I picture an assembly line of Henry Ford (he's another one) where they were putting certain brainpower "under the hood." When they came to me, it was decided to give me the basic "four cylinder" - not a lot of power but just enough to get to the grocery store and bank and do the necessary chores.

But being a "K.I.S.S." (Keep It Simple, Saint) can have its perks. I really can't plumb the depths that some of the brainiacs frequent. It's led to a simple faith. I see clearly that God made His existence and character basic enough so that heaven isn't only reserved for those eight-cylinder guys.

The basic component of The First Person of The Trinity is that He cares for us. That's pretty simple.

God made sure Adam and Eve had all the answers they needed through a simple walk in the cool of the day with their heavenly Father.

## PORTAL TO HEAVEN

Jesus made sure people had all the answers they needed by telling them about His dad, showing them eternity's compassion and righteousness and inviting even the little children and simpletons to come to Him. Even a four-cylinder guy has his advantages on this drive to heaven.

*Where is the wise person? Where is the teacher of the law? Where is the philosopher of this age? Has not God made foolish the wisdom of the world? For since in the wisdom of God the world through its wisdom did not know him, God was pleased through the foolishness of what was preached to save those who believe...*

**1 Corinthians 1:27 (NIV)**

There is intentionality when a couple celebrates their love in intimacy even when it's ignited unintentionally! But another intentionality may go beyond passion. "You thinking what I'm thinking? Let's make a baby."

When that baby arrives, a mystical union between those two lovers expands and it is within this context that the parents wonder, "Who will this child become?" The succeeding years are spent developing all manner of potential. But when a kid isn't conceived in a true love nest, he or she may have a harder time conceiving the purpose for which they were conceived. And if a father or mother or both abandon a child, who is left to rise to the occasion or open themselves up for homework, coaching, teaching or simply cuddling or hugging?

While working at a prison, I noticed without exception that the young inmates were angry that they weren't really wanted; they just "happened" and were purposeless.

## ᴘORTAL ᴛO ʜEAVEN

This overall inequity was that even in the cases of rape or selfish and irresponsible acts, God was still "breeding" life, true God-breathed life for the taking. The unholy can be used by our holy Father. This is the great metaphor of hope for so much of life in general. There's an intentionality in God's design despite man's irresponsible unintentionality.

*But to as many as did receive and welcome Him, He gave the authority (power, privilege, right) to become the children of God, that is, to those who believe in (adhere to, trust in, and rely on) His name—who owe their birth neither to bloods nor to the will of the flesh [that of physical impulse] nor to the will of man [that of a natural father], but to God. [They are born of God!]*

**John 1:12,13 (AMPC)**

If a relationship with God as our father was solely dependent upon our experiences with our dads, many would not be able to enter the kingdom of God.

For what of the fatherless or those who had less-than-perfect dads who were workaholics, alcoholics, abusers, adulterers, self-absorbed, hobbyists, road warriors, introverts, insensitive to their wives, godless and who knows what else. If "father-wounds" prevented us from truly understanding the father-healing heart of God, we wouldn't even know where to find Father's Day on a calendar.

Sometimes, God will give us a "second father" here on earth who clearly demonstrates the character of God. My dad died earlier in my life and an older man stepped into that role. I encourage others to seek out someone like that – no matter your age!

But a lot of my discoveries of fatherhood happened after the hospital nurse handed my firstborn to me. An instinctive father-heart began to beat and I gained a hyper-sensitivity to the way God was raising me. For by this time, my earthly dad had joined my Heavenly one. It was just Father God and myself. Through my sins of omission, commission and outright rebellion, I received correction and continuous grace and mercy from Father God. I really couldn't look my children in the eye and give them anything less.

## PORTAL TO HEAVEN

God re-fathered me. Whether it's through children, a parental role-model or some other way, He will do the same for you. Moreover, He gave His Son so we could see our true DNA.

*Anyone who has seen me has seen the Father. How can you say,*
*'Show us the Father?'*

**John 14:9 (NIV)**

It's a hot July day on the Jersey shore and I'm leaning on the railing of the second floor of the beach pavilion surveying hundreds on the boardwalk. Out of these countless locals and tourists, I spot my daughter and my grandchildren.

How do they stand out in such a vast crowd?

It's father-radar. When you've been watching over a child's every move since they were born, you get a sense of where "they're at."

From that second-floor vantage, I had the perspective of looking down. If I was at eye level, I wouldn't have been able to see them through the masses.

Between these convergent factors of a birds-eye-view and father-radar, it's easier to understand God's ability to know us intimately.

While we will never have the perfect perspective of others the way only God can, we can get a measure of how He cares for each one of us.

## ᏢORTAL ᏟTO ᎻEAVEN

Only God truly knows where "we are at" – spiritually and geographically. In that sense, there's no such thing as a bored-walk.

*You know my sitting down and my rising up; You understand my thought afar off.*

**Psalm 139:2 (NIV)**

The smell of urine on the seat of his wheelchair was substantially noticeable. The trick was to not make it seem noticeable.

That was probably the noble, lifelong duty of Jim's Vietnam veteran friend who accompanied him every three months to my office. The friend had smelled and seen much worse.

Exam rooms can get pretty intimate and the plenteous nature of the odor mixed with the constraints of the 9 by 12-foot space was only intensified because of the size of the wheelchair. We were like sardines, only those fish smelled better.

I asked the friend how he had come to care so deeply for his cerebral palsy buddy.

"We got history," was his short-but-friendly reply.

It made me think of God's relationship with Israel. The Lord knew the nation from infancy, through childhood and adolescence and into the adult years. In short, they had history.

The offensive odors of the country's rebellion didn't seem to phase the Lord's longsuffering.

## PORTAL TO HEAVEN

God also has history with us. He knows when we wheel in with suffering, heartache, sin and even a wet and extremely noticeable adult diaper. It's very likely that the patient faithfulness of Jim's friend was an office visit for me rather than for Jim.

*He is God, the faithful God, who keeps His covenant and His lovingkindness to a thousandth generation with those who love Him and keep His commandments...*

**Deuteronomy 7:9 (NIV)**

One of the many mirrors in life is a sibling...

A nice thing about having a brother on the west coast is that late-night desires for a phone conversation are still fair game when you take into consideration the three-hour time difference.

The evening is when life creeps up on our vulnerability. Weariness, a sore back, an unproductive or disappointing day or the prospect of a difficult tomorrow can all be in the mix for a chat rather than a pillow.

That's when I pick up the phone and call my brother. Whenever he's able, he'll field the call.

An hour later, I hear him say, "I think you're ready for bed – I can hear it in your voice." He's usually caught me during long stretches of listening and he can tell that I'm nodding on the phone.

Everyone needs a brother or sister like him whether related by blood or not. This would be a person with whom you've grown up and who knows you inside and out.

Facetime and cell phones have conquered the distance challenge.

## PORTAL TO HEAVEN

Prayer is a lot like a late-night long-distance phone conversation - but at any time of the day. The one on the other end of the line knows us so well.

*...The LORD is near to all who call on him, to all who call on him in truth.... the soul of Jonathan was knit to the soul of David, and Jonathan loved him as his own soul...*

**Psalm 145:18 (ESV), 1 Samuel 18:1 (ESV)**

Knowing someone closely is one of the greatest privileges on earth. Simply put, it's a window into the very heart of God.

If there is a softness of soul within a friend or lover, we get a glimpse of our God who fashioned us to reflect His tenderness.

If someone exudes a determined spirit, it helps us rest in the security of a Father who will fight for us and never leave us no matter how determined we are to drift from Him.

A spouse who is sincere and trustworthy reminds us that Jesus is only and always truth itself. He or she will never betray and always exhibits the loyalty of one willing to lay down their life. The contrast of that love with the backstabbing of the world helps cement our trust in God.

And what of laughter? Those who make us chuckle help us understand that the world does not rest on our shoulders.

Knowing someone deeply not only tells us something about the character of God. It gives us a view of our soul – sometimes by contrast and sometimes through their role as a spiritual mate of sorts.

Perhaps a consistent holy gaze into each other's eyes might remind us that we are made in the image of God.

## PORTAL TO HEAVEN

The privilege of knowing someone really well is a way that God shows us that we can have this same privilege with our Creator Father, his incredible "knowable" Son and the partnership of His Holy Spirit.

*Then God said, 'Let Us make man in Our image, according to Our likeness...'*

**Genesis 1:26 (NASB)**

You're eager to catch up on the happenings in the lives of cousins and friends. Yet, the clock is ticking on this reunion and you know everyone will be leaving shortly.

In some sense, that's what our "visit" to earth is like. The "thrower of the party" is God and we have a select amount of time to get to know Him.

It would be expected that everyone at the affair would be lined up to talk with this host. Interestingly, Jesus says it is not so. He tells those within earshot that "narrow is the way" and few take advantage. He says that the cares of this world pick-off so many.

In an era and cultures that invite distraction with abundant pleasures, it is easy to see how Jesus could turn into a wallflower at his own party. He is too loving for that.

...The birds wake me up in the morning as if on assignment. They are relentless until I succumb and stand despite the pleasures of sleep.

Whether it's birds or the two year-old who spins in her new dress or the sunset that reflects in your rear-view mirror or Julie Andrews singing, "Getting to Know You," there is a God who is the pursuing wallflower.

## ᏢORTAL ᏟO ᎻEAVEN

God's constant invitation awaits around every bend: "Awake, you are invited to get to know Me at a limited-time gathering. Please R.S.V.P. as soon as possible."

*Jesus replied: 'A certain man was preparing a great banquet and invited many guests...But they all alike began to make excuses'
...Christ's love compels us...*

**Luke 14:16ff (NIV), 2 Corinthians 5:14 (NIV)**

Riding my bike where I have never ridden it before, I am disappointed and nearly outraged when I look down on the ground.

It is loaded with mulberries.

Mulberries I could have picked. Mulberry-picking-season I should have put on my calendar. Mulberry regret.

It's a quick snap-shot of my life. Could-have's and should-have's and their accompanying regret grind my soul at times.

Yet, when I take my eye off the ground and look up at the mulberry tree, I find it is still loaded. Again, it's a picture of my life. Either I look down at and see what I have missed or I look up and see what I still have – and where I should be concentrating my efforts.

## ΡORTAL ϹTO ϤEAVEN

We live in the present…I pull out my smart phone and put it on the calendar. The little people in my life will love this outing. And when I see their purple hands, mouths and tongues, I will have no regrets.

*…one thing I do, forgetting those things which are behind and reaching forward to those things which are ahead, I press toward the goal for the prize of the upward call of God in Christ Jesus.*

**Philippians 3:13,14 (NKJV)**

I had eaten a little too much. To work it off, I decided to go for a bike ride.

I almost bumped my head on a low-hanging branch loaded with mulberries. I had forgotten the tight little window of the Mulberry Tree. They come and they go. Last year, I had gotten out of there too late.

If I hadn't overeaten, I wouldn't have taken the bike out for some exercise. If I hadn't almost hit that branch…ah, the if's.

Sometimes, I wish I had more deliberately taken some other "trails" in life and yet here I was benefitting from some serendipitous path and all because I had a full belly that led me to a fuller trail.

A great writer and Pulitzer-Prize winner once consoled me with these words after I told him that I wished I had made writing a career. "Two ships leave the same port and sail different seas and return to the same port."

I am not suggesting that planning is a waste of time. But what do we make of strings of "coincidence" and tail winds that get us back to the same port as fast as our friends who took different routes – and often just as fast or quicker?

## PORTAL TO HEAVEN

Despite my own ponderings about destiny and sovereignty,
I truly believe Someberry is looking out for me no matter which
boat or trail I take.

*[Jesus said] 'And by a coincidence a certain priest was going down along that road'… The race is not to the swift or the battle to the strong, nor does food come to the wise or wealth to the brilliant or favor to the learned; but time and chance happen to them all… The eyes of the LORD are in every place, Watching the evil and the good.*

**Lk 10:31, (YLT), Ec 9:11 (NIV), Pr 15:3 (NASB)**

Our Mulberry Tree is loaded. I found myself wanting to hoard.

Why should the birds eat from my tree? I see them pecking away without the need for my binoculars. No sense trying to hide, you greedy little guys.

To make matters worse, I hear my wife exclaim, "Isn't he cute?"

Jealously, I look out to see if a twenty-four year-old GQ model-type in a hard hat got lost after looking down a trench too long. No. It's a bear "cutely" standing on his hind legs eating these tiny purple tasties with these huge paws.

And then it hit me. I didn't plant that tree. I didn't tend it. I can't even understand why it's such a bumper year and I sure couldn't have thought up the idea of mulberries. I reserve that for Someone else I know: "Look! I have given you every seed-bearing plant throughout the earth and all the fruit trees for your food…" (Genesis 1:29)

## ΡORTAL ΤO ΗEAVEN

It was pretty easy to have a desire for that tree. Reminds us of another scenario in Genesis.

*The woman was convinced. She saw that the tree was beautiful and its fruit looked delicious, and she wanted the wisdom it would give her. So she took some of the fruit and ate it.*

**Genesis 3:6 (NLT)**

We have some very mature mulberry trees that grace our property and they are pregnant with possibilities. I want to get some kids over here and see their delight as they stuff their faces with no one saying, "Hey, put that back on the counter." Well, this is better than the candy aisle anyway.

I've already had mulberry pancakes several days in a row and mulberries seem to be brimming over my granola and I am now envisioning cobbler or pies or just walking by and reaching my hand up with my eyes closed.

However, potential, as delicious as it can be, is not a certain thing. So, we wish and work for that which we cannot see and remember past seasons when potential became reality.

## PORTAL TO HEAVEN

When we go through dry times, this mulberry metaphor triggers hope from former times when we had plenty of loaded trees. We appreciate the "loaded" times and be patient when the "dry" times visit. Berry nice.

*Hope deferred makes the heart sick, But desire fulfilled is a tree of life.*

**Proverbs 13:12 (ESV)**

I had been wondering why the deer were hanging out in our side yard with their heads to the ground. I happened to be over there and inadvertently found my answer lying all over the ground.

Our Mulberry Tree was dropping berries like candy out of a piñata. I was a bit disturbed. After all, that's a gigantic waste.

Someone recently said, "Hey, the animals and birds have to eat, too." It was right out of The Bible: "Your heavenly Father feeds them." I conceded.

It brought to mind God's benevolence.

Here I was thinking of purple pancakes, the dye-like hands and mouths of our little people and the fun of lining up my ladder to see just how high I could get up on the tree.

## PORTAL TO HEAVEN

Obviously, God's benevolence is higher than my view from the top of any ladder. Deer me.

*Look at the birds of the air, for they neither sow nor reap nor gather into barns; yet your heavenly Father feeds them... The young lions roar after their prey and seek their food from God.*

**Matthew 6:26 (NKJV), Psalm 104:21(NIV)**

# July

## PORTALS TO HEAVEN

Desperately searching for a Fourth of July celebration on the Jersey Shore, I hit on a great website that has more fireworks than places where Washington supposedly slept.

The obvious reason there were so many selections is the curve of the earth. If it was a little flatter, we could all just have one big bang.

This all leads me to wonder about the fireworks surrounding the return of Jesus. I'm sure He's got it figured out, but with twenty-four time zones, how does everyone see Him at once. Is there a time delay? Is it like a visit from The Pope where it's more of a tour? Is there something that instantaneously happens in the minds and hearts of 7 billion people? Is everyone led to their televisions or computers simultaneously and it's carried live? Lots of flatscreens?

Who could figure the timing or the logistics of the return of Jesus Christ?

## PORTAL TO HEAVEN

Most towns and cities plan and prepare and use their great resources to coordinate holiday celebrations. May we be part of those who help bring our communities to the point of preparation for the fireworks surrounding the majestic return of Jesus Christ.

*Then the kingdom of heaven shall be likened to ten virgins who took their lamps and went out to meet the bridegroom. Now five of them were wise, and five were foolish... 'Watch therefore, for you know neither the day nor the hour in which the Son of Man is coming.'*

**Matthew 25:1,2,13 (NKJV)**

Emotions during the Fourth of July fireworks over The Hudson River near Lady Liberty range from pride to awe. Television cameras zoom in on tear-streamed faces.

It makes your mind go in two directions: backward and forward. Thinking about America's history, we see that the founding fathers had stars in their eyes as well as in their flag.

They sought and fought for a country free from an unrighteous king where the people would reign through a democratic system that would somehow be fair for all.

History has never seen anything work that well nor has any country prospered like The United States.

And yet now, there seems to be a second revolution over what constitutes equity. Still others want to import a different system with a whole new set of underlying beliefs. America has changed from a "melting pot" to a boiling pot.

Beneath many arguments in our country is the elephant in the room: the Man Jesus. It's a subtle silence. Scripture warns that a country that ignores God will find itself in trouble. While tussles repeat over fairness, the real debates should be fixed on how closely we are following God and His word.

## ᑭORTAL ᒍO ᕼEAVEN

Christ has always been the elephant in the room. In Scripture, Jesus is referred to as the "scandalon" or the stone that makes men stumble or the rock that an individual and country build upon.

*...this stone [Christ] is precious. But to those who do not believe, 'The stone the builders rejected has become the cornerstone,' and, 'A stone of stumbling and a rock'... Unless the Lord builds the house, those who build it labor in vain. Unless the Lord watches over the city, the watchman stays awake in vain.*

**1 Peter 2:7,8, (BSB), Psalm 127:1 (ESV)**

Images abound when someone hears Ray Charles sing "America The Beautiful." It could be of fruited plains, purple mountains, wondrous natural resources, the crashing of the waves against the rocky coasts, spacious skies, volunteer firemen, heroes long buried, founding fathers, great presidents, Rockwell's Main Street citizens, etc., etc.

Why do I get a lump in my throat during the singing of the national anthem before the athletes of our national pastime take the field? Is it because Dorothy was right? "There's no place like home." What makes America beautiful? What makes anything beautiful?

We get our looks from our parents. So the natural question is, "Who is America's father?" There was a time when the unanimous or nearly unanimous answer would be, " God." Our money speaks of this answer: "In God we trust."

If we are God's children, we should craft our laws and behaviors around His expressed will in the scriptures.

## PORTAL TO HEAVEN

May we respond to Ray Charles' call for help in singing about our true Founding Father during his version of "America The Beautiful:"

"But now wait a minute, I'm talking about
America, sweet America,
You know, God done shed his grace on thee,
He crowned thy good, yes he did, in a brotherhood,
From sea to shining sea.
You know, I wish I had somebody to help me sing this…"

*Blessed is the nation whose God is the Lord, whose people
he has chosen as his own.*

**Psalm 33:12 (NLT)**

"There are no red or blue states," shouts the politician seconds before he skewers the "other" party.

This is nothing new. Abraham Lincoln recognized this problem in his famous senatorial acceptance speech known for his borrowing of scripture: "A house divided against itself cannot stand." In some sense, a divided country is simply the bigger picture of what happens in our own lives.

Anyone who has lived in a home or worked in a business or chatted in a high school hallway knows the insidious and nerve-wracking sensation when division rules.

These personal experiences only serve to make us extra sensitive when it comes to the church. Many of us have witnessed minor and major church splits.

And what of the greater church? At last count, the list of denominations ranged from over 200 to nearly 50,000 - depending upon your definition of a denomination.

But just like the churches, there are hair-splitting differences within differences. Such minute conflicts begin as a cordial Independence Day picnic tug-of-war and end up rope-burning the hands of everyone.

## PORTAL TO HEAVEN

It would be wise to rather choose a follow-the-leader game at our Fourth of July outings that include the wisdom that Lincoln directly borrowed from the leader:

*Every kingdom divided against itself is brought to desolation, and every city or house divided against itself will not stand.*

**(Jesus Christ, as recorded in Matthew 12:25)**

"America, America, God shed His…"

A gentleman who volunteers with World War II and Korean veterans sadly relayed these words: "They all tell me the same thing," he said forlornly, " 'This is not my country anymore.' "

What would make them say that? Where did America go wrong?

Are these vets talking about the 1960's and all the freedom that the younger generation thought they were bringing to the backward old-timers? Are these "old-timers" being influenced by what they see on television? Is it shocking their senses more than the mortars they endured?

It must be heartbreaking to believe that all that sacrifice was for naught. But even the "greatest generation" cannot free the tangled sin within the human heart.

The Bible spells it out. When the letters are red, things get even simpler.

For example, when Jesus was being challenged, He answered simply: "So Jesus said to the Jews who had believed him, 'If you abide in my word, you are truly my disciples, and you will know the truth, and the truth will set you free.… everyone who practices sin is a slave to sin.' " (John 8:31,32)

## PORTAL TO HEAVEN

While soldiers like the "greatest generation" fought for the freedom from the enemies of state, Jesus' contest was with the greatest foe and his walk matched his talk; both in red.

*[Jesus] purchased our freedom and forgave our sins.*

**Colossians 1:14 (NLT)**

# PEN YOUR PORTALS

Before I received Christ as Lord and Savior and began to understand his kingdom, I measured and saw things through the eyes of the world's system and Satan's rules - or should I say his "out-laws." But when I was "born-again" into His kingdom, I was given a new heart and new eyes.

There are times when I either literally or figuratively see things of heaven represented by things of earth.

For instance, Christ said that we enter the kingdom of God like a child. So God has given me children and their offspring to show me how a child acts. I lead. They follow. Is this not one of the simplest portals to heaven?

Jesus used everyday experiences and metaphors. And speaking of little ones, He used babies to explain the born-again experience to Israel's most sophisticated teacher when he told Nicodemus: "You must be born again to enter the kingdom of God...If I have told you earthly things and you do not believe, how will you believe if I tell you of heavenly things?" (John 3:12) Later, the great Jewish rabbi sensitively helped bury Jesus after the resurrection. Now, that's beholding.

## PORTAL TO HEAVEN

Glimpses, and deliberate ones at that, lead to beholding. Practice makes perfect.

*Nicodemus brought a mixture of myrrh...*

**John 19:39 (NIV)**

I've been tired. I even wake up exhausted. I have a lot on my mind. Perhaps because the head is on top of the body, it weighs down my physique when the skull is carrying more burdens than was intended.

Light has a way of waking us up. This is the case this morning. I look out the window. It is a beautiful sunrise that sneakily is getting more gorgeous with each tweet of our ebullient birds. It's as if our little winged creatures are getting so excited by the light that they are screaming, "Wake up! Wake up!"

### ᑭORTAL ᑕTO ᕼEAVEN

Light, particularly that of the sunrise, is the antidote to the darkness of weariness, discouragement and the weight of the world on the shoulders that emanates from our heads.

*Give your burdens to the LORD, and he will take care of you. ... In him was life, and that life was the light of all mankind. The light shines in the darkness, and the darkness has not overcome it. ... The one who is the true light, who gives light to everyone, was coming into the world.*

**1 Peter 5:7 (NLT), John 1:4,5 (NIV), John 1:9 (NLT)**

I'm in the basement. A little messy. A little musty. A little of this and, believe me, a little of that. The ceiling is low. I've heard more than one person swear after hitting their heads on a waste pipe.

Then, I look out through the Bilco cellar door and view that it's beautiful outside. I see my wisteria-covered well house. Those lavender clusters are as lovely as anything Monet could have put in the middle of his garden.

There is no ceiling out there for the eagle to bang his bald head on. No Truman-Show canopy for an airplane to hit.

## PORTAL TO HEAVEN

Are we sentenced to a musty and messy incarceration because we are not looking through the portals to heaven?

*'No eye has seen, and no ear has heard, and no mind has imagined the things which God has prepared for those who love him.'*

**1 Corinthians 2:9 (NHEB)**

I'm monkeying around behind the fence of my pool and things are not going well. I bleed the filter. I change my baskets. I check the deep-water valve. I stare at the pressure gage. Dang. Still low.

I turn off the power switch. I backwash the system. There's something wrong and I can't figure it out and I lose my patience.

Then, suddenly, I look through a small hole in the fence and I see the sparkling blue water in my pool just a few feet from me. I think of the little ones splashing me and diving in the deep end. Water guns, our perennial inflatable "Albert-the-alligator" and a few laps when I'm alone...lying on my back and watching the clouds go by. I'm inspired to keep the working on the pool system.

## ꝑORTAL ꞇO ꞕEAVEN

On one side of the fence, I fret and fuss and figure. But on the other side of this mechanical suffering is an entire summer of joy. The metaphor of earth and heaven lies before me through a hole in the fence.

*For I consider that the sufferings of this present time are not worth comparing with the glory that is to be revealed to us.*

**Romans 8:18 (ESV)**

I pull into the parking space in front of the Holiday Inn. I am not expecting much.

The price seemed a little too reasonable for this popular resort area with its ideal climate.

The building is unimpressive. The pool has a chain-link fence around it. The walk-up to the second floor resembles a modest apartment complex.

Suddenly, I see through the stairway to the 9th hole and it's beautifully and mysteriously inviting.

## PORTAL TO HEAVEN

Pre-judgments can close portals to heaven. It's a holiday and I'm inn.

*Don't jump to conclusions...*
*'Do not judge by appearances, but judge with right judgment.'*

**Proverbs 25:18 (The Message), John 7:24, (ESV)**

I witness the sunrise most mornings. It's like the Son. It dawned on me that the sun keeps coming up each morning whether or not I've contributed to deepening this world's long dark night or if I've made it a light-er burden for others.

The Son doesn't reserve his rising for when we've been good little boys and girls. If we were to project conditional love onto seven billion people, the sun would never come up. God doesn't withhold His heart just because we break it.

While we must guard ourselves about unnecessary pain that may come through others (picture deliberately walking down a dark alley at night), we can make our way through life with the grace of the risen Son for those who injure us. Forgiveness truly is the summation of the Christian faith.

There are songs and posters that convey the sentiment that we should "love like we've never been hurt." Why is that so easy to dismiss as the kind of plaque-mush found in tourist gift shops? It's the very wall art that Jesus, on vacation of course, would stop, show to His Father, and ask, "I'd like to buy this one."

"Sure, Son," would be the reply.

## PORTAL TO HEAVEN

Borrowing from God's daily sunrise metaphor, I must awaken while it's still dark, roll out of bed and brighten a day of someone who has been wounded or who has hurt me.

*'I tell you, [forgive] not seven times, but seventy-seven times.'*

**Jesus as recorded in Matthew 18:22 (NIV) [Editor's brackets]**

One of the biggest regrets that worry-warts will have after their death will be when they look through their lifelong-log of anxieties. Here they will find on the inside front cover an inscription that will either make them furious or give them an incurable case of ironic laughter: "I have spent most of my life worrying about things that have never happened. Signed, Mark Twain."

Worrying is like blowing a million bucks on something that doesn't work. I wonder if we're all like Mark Twain and have to stumble upon this truth only after living most of our life to come to this conclusion. My late spiritual mentor was fond of saying, "When you figure out how to construct or fix everything in your house, it will be time to move." Maybe it will be time to move out of this physical home by the time we "fix" all the worry repairs of our lives.

## PORTAL TO HEAVEN

By observing God's faithfulness in our lives, we train ourselves to break this vicious and wasteful habit of worry. First step: journal all of worries - big and small. Start by listing all of the ones that have plagued you from childhood. If Twain is right, you will see in black and white that you've been worrying about things that never happened. Next, write down all of the worries that you can think of for the present and the future.

Let an insightful person whom you respect see your journal and see if he or she helps confirm Twain's conclusion.

*So don't worry about these things, saying, 'What will we eat? What will we drink? What will we wear?' These things dominate the thoughts of unbelievers, but your heavenly Father already knows all your needs.*

**Matthew 6:31,32 (NLT)**

"I have spent most of my life worrying about things that have never happened." Mark Twain

Twain could have added that it's almost sacrilegious for a Christian to think and speak words of worry – except that Twain would have said it in more sarcastic way.

Sometimes when we think or pray about our needs, we go to God as if He'd be surprised that our rent or mortgage or student loan or homework assignment is due on the first of the month. What does this attitude say about the way we view God's character?

Eating, drinking, clothing, homes, etc. These are things that are necessary. Wouldn't God be pretty mean if He didn't provide directly or indirectly for our needs?

## PORTAL TO HEAVEN

God has provided for us and has thereby proved His faithfulness.

While mankind's leaders have often withheld provision to their citizens through mismanagement, wars and power plays, our righteous king has provided plenty of resources to take care of all of the people on this planet.

*For your heavenly Father knows that you need all these things. But seek first the kingdom of God and His righteousness, and all these things shall be added to you… God is not a man, that He should lie, Nor a son of man, that He should repent. Has He said, and will He not do?*
*Or has He spoken, and will He not make it good?*

**Matthew 6:32,33 (NKJV)Numbers 23:19 (NKJV)**

The news media is like a worldwide virus when it comes to worry. If these agitators can get us on the edge of our seats by throttling bad news our way, they can probably get us to tune in tomorrow for another round of suspense as to whether a terrorist attack or worldwide recession is going to happen...soon...like tomorrow.

They funnel news slowly as in a soap opera that always ends on a sour note; a clever strategy for selling advertisements.

Without ignoring local and worldwide concerns, counter the anxieties that the news outlets purvey by "tuning in" The Good News and you will find this headline: *"So do not worry about tomorrow; for tomorrow will care for itself. Each day has enough trouble of its own."* *Matthew 6:33

## ᖯORTAL ᏨᎢO ᕼEAVEN

The Word of God is an antidote. He promises to be near to those who draw near to Him. When little children get near their parents, they feel more secure and less anxious.

*I will stand my watch and set myself on the rampart, and watch to see what He will say to me, and what I will answer when I am corrected. Then the Lord answered me and said: 'Write the vision and make it plain on tablets...the just shall live by faith.'*

**Habakkuk 2:1,2,4 (NKJV)**

I know that none of you worry. So, I'll just talk (write) to myself.

Take money, for instance. I concern myself with this from time to time. Once in a while. Once a month. Perhaps every week. Maybe more like daily.

The interesting thing is that it doesn't have anything to do with whether I have money or not. I've worried about money when finding a quarter on a sidewalk was a huge blessing. "The skies opened up," I'd think.

But when the heavens poured with prosperity, I still got concerned. "It could disappear, you know," I said to myself.

And then, when I had a windfall, it was like fear of heights. I was timid of success and a bit nervous that I might squander it like 20-point lead in the fourth quarter.

Worry doesn't have anything to do with finances or the future or any other thing. It has to do with fear.

The Apostle of Love, John, says that perfect love casts out all fear because fear has to do with punishment and that usually is about "our performance" versus God's provision in any area of our lives.

## PORTAL TO HEAVEN

Our worry blocks heaven itself and proves that we don't really understand God's motivation. Picture a loving father with his young one on his knee. The father may wear a belt, but when they are in unison, the only thing the child sees is the apple of his father's eye as reflected in those same eyes.

*Jesus... 'If you knew me, you would know my Father also.'*

**John 8:19 (NIV)**

I have obsessive tendencies when it comes to sunrises. I think it's a clever strategy of The Maker of Sunrises to get my butt out of bed.

Could it be He knows about propensities for rest, comfort, security, shelter and all the other things that a bed affords. There appears to be a larger lesson here. Is it that He knows that grand interruptions are the only way to get our attention? Picture a teenager on a Saturday morning when Dad wants some help with the yard and he's waited long enough. Or what about the college kid trying to sleep-off Friday night and his engineering-major-roommate decides to pull the curtain back to get some homework done.

There's always a temptation to sleep-off our dark troubles and the expectations and responsibilities of life. So, God hires a big yellow ball to shine some light on these issues.

God's real genius in garnering my attention first thing in the morning is that weariness, pain and problems are overshadowed by His utter beauty. Think marriage here. The same wife who writes the "Honey-Do" list is the one that the husband stares at while she is sleeping. At least she offers a legitimately enticing reason *not* to get out of bed.

## ᏢORTAL ᏟO ᎮEAVEN

Juxtaposition is a favorite tactic of a very, very clever waker-upper God.

*The Master, God, has given me a well-taught tongue, So I know how to encourage tired people. He wakes me up in the morning, Wakes me up, opens my ears to listen as one ready to take orders. The Master, God, opened my ears, and I didn't go back to sleep, didn't pull the covers back over my head.*

**Isaiah 50:4,5 (The Message)**

There are times when a portal to heaven comes in a near-literal manner through a break in the clouds.

Sometimes there are streams of sunbeams that portend a more radiant light; one that we have not experienced yet. It's the kind that is described by those who have had near-death experiences. These folks have all seen light before they see Christ.

On those days when a cloud gets poked by heaven, I can flatly say, "Gee, we're finally getting a break in the weather." Or, I can say, "There's my portal to heaven. Can't wait to see all of it."

One time, I had to walk off a heavy dinner…conversation, that is. It was one in which my heart had been misconstrued. As the sun was setting across the field, a small opening in the clouds seemed to say, "It's just a glimmer." It was symbolic and it was literal. We only get a "ray" of hope down here. Sometimes, that's enough to salvage some "heart" burn.

## PORTAL TO HEAVEN

These clouds can be like the obvious hints that parents leave behind during Easter-egg hunts.

*It came about, however, when the congregation had assembled against Moses and Aaron, that they turned toward the tent of meeting, and behold, the cloud covered it and the glory of the LORD appeared.*

**Numbers 16:42 (NAS)**

"Everybody talks about the weather, but nobody seems to do anything about it." (Charles Dudley Warner)

I actually like watching weather. It keeps me looking up. But I also find it fascinating that around the 25,000 spherical miles of this globe, weather is happening in every one of those miles whether anyone wants to do something about it. (Think, "It's raining on our parade.")

Beyond that, it's bedeviling trying to predict it. I was driving with a friend who is a meteorologist and we went through a downpour with scary lightening all around us. When I pulled into my driveway, there wasn't a puddle. The meteorologist looked as confused as me.

## PORTAL TO HEAVEN

Weather can be generalized in this most profound conclusion: "Man proposes, God disposes." Meteorology is one of the greatest tangible examples of the power and control of God over this earth; all 25,000 spherical miles AND each of its inhabitants...if they are smart enough to look up. Notwithstanding, parades and picnics are still kind of fun to try and plan.

*Come now, you who say, 'Today or tomorrow we will go to such and such a city, and spend a year there and engage in business and make a profit.' Yet you do not know what your life will be like tomorrow. You are just a vapor that appears for a little while and then vanishes away. Instead, you ought to say, 'If the Lord wills, we will live and also do this or that.'...*

**James 4:13-15 (ESV)**

Beauty is in the eye of the beholder and everyone has a different idea of what a "perfect day" should look like.

The where and when are only the cherry on the top. The deliciousness of a perfect day to me is spending time with my family and extracting as much unity and joy as possible.

Another portal to heaven is a day at the beach with the grown kids and little kids and a perfect sunrise to start the morning.

I had been wondering if something as nebulous as a "perfect day" would be considered tangible enough for most to understand as a portal to heaven. I say this because there is not necessarily a moment in time, but rather a splat of impressionism on a 24-hour painting. But then I got my confirmation as I opened a letter from a ministry whose heart I adore. It read, "It was a perfect day. And those don't come along very often; they come by invitation only." I would add that it's often a surprise invitation as well.

This trip down to the Jersey shore started with both surprise and invitation. My daughter casually mentioned, "Hey dad, we're going down the shore. Would you like to come?"

Bingo. Surprise. Invitation. Family. Perfect day.

## PORTAL TO HEAVEN
Beauty is in the eyes of the sender of all beauty.

*Many, LORD my God, are the wonders you have done, the things you planned for us. None can compare with you; were I to speak and tell of your deeds, they would be too many to declare.*

**Psalm 40:5 (NIV)**

My architectural love for Victorians stems back from growing up in one and in their sheer beauty. They were constructed to comfortably fit a family of nine, and ten occasionally. You know, back in the day.

First, there's the Victorian witch's hat or "turret" as it is called. It's the most prominent feature. It points straight up to the sky as if the architect knew about portals to heaven.

But smallness also makes a home and the realities of urban living and tighter economies are making "little" both hip and creative. There's also the very square spin: the no-frills modular where we raised our kids. It was the farthest thing from a Victorian. I loved it because of family, friends and the memories. A neighbor once gave me a card with a poem about the bigness of the love in our little home.

And what of that classic little bungalow at the ocean-side tourist town? These were the original beach houses. They can have little variations that make them stand out. In fact, in the shore town of Ocean Grove, New Jersey, there are units that don't get much smaller: tiny white tents from Methodist camp meetings over a hundred years ago. Though small, they can be creative. Some even leave the flaps open so a passerby can view their homey feel.

## PORTAL TO HEAVEN

The ideal perfect-home square "footage" lies in the shoes at the front door.

*In my Father's house are many mansions: if it were not so, I would have told you. I go to prepare a place for you.*

**John 14:2 (KJV)**

# August
## PORTALS
## TO HEAVEN

My daughter let her new kitten out of her apartment. She was afraid that the larger, more mature cats would bully him. To her surprise, "Mowgli" ended up cornering the neighborhood bully within a few moments. My daughter was suddenly kind of proud that her baby could not only take care of himself, but he was the big jock on the team.

Perspective. Fairness. It can all change very rapidly.

I think I could conjure up some great psychology studies by giving some subjects the upper hand one day and swapping their role the next. It's kind of like Monopoly. You love when players land on you're your property, but think the game is unfair and pity yourself as ill-used when you land on the hotel of your opponent – especially when it's sunny at the beach and you were just sauntering down the BOARDWALK.

We are like chameleons. We often react to life from whatever vantage point we find ourselves.

If we're white, we don't like discrimination when we pay more tuition than the non-white applicant. If we are not white, it might be tempting to think we should get an edge – one that the whites had cornered the market on for eons.

## PORTAL TO HEAVEN

There's only one way to skin a cat (sorry, Mowgli)…be on the side of God who always operates in fairness – whether our kid or kitty is Number 1 or on the bottom rung.

*For there is no partiality with God.*

**Romans 2:11 (NAS)**

I went to a high school where there were only two African American kids in my 200-plus graduating class.

I liked being white because I was who I was. Period. I particularly liked being of Italian American descent despite a few disparaging jokes now and then about my ethnicity and the New Jersey mob. The ironic thing was these comments were tossed about by ethnic-ers who had previously been the butt of the punch lines by some other group, race or creed. And on and on it goes.

I never considered myself a snob or prejudiced because I was white. In fact, I always thought I was hip, or at the very least lucky, because I had friends of different nationalities, religions and races. But then it happened. A Jewish friend whose family had narrowly escaped the Holocaust told me that anyone who says they are not prejudiced in some way is a "liar." I never asked him where his biases lay.

"Dad," my daughter once told me. "My generation is color-blind. Yours isn't."

After being on and off the short-term mission field for nearly twenty years, I can tell you that being white in non-white countries does open your eyes. And world statistics that tell me that I am the minority on this spinning globe.

## PORTAL TO HEAVEN

Grow daily in the knowledge that God deliberately made the races. It's probably part of His vast, seven-billion-people, 196-nation conspiracy to help us see with His eyes.

*Then Peter began to speak: 'I now realize how true it is that God does not show favoritism but accepts from every nation the one who fears him and does what is right.'*

**Acts 10:34, 35 (NIV)**

Full disclosure: I am white. Also, full disclosure here: I was born that way. Worse full disclosure: I am a white American.

This puts me at a tremendous disadvantage with regard to some of the perspectives of The God who made me white.

I am not talking about the applications that might not give a son or daughter an edge on a college or employment application. I am talking street-level, guttural stuff.

As I've grown older, I realized that I was missing a lot of the perspective of non-whites. And I am not just talking about the financially disadvantaged. Like a left-hand layup in basketball or a back-hand in tennis or my times-tables, racial perspective actually takes time and effort – especially from those of us who grew up in the white burbs, attended white schools and worked around white coworkers. Leaving that bubble is a little like getting off the The Lazy Boy after a beer and chips and a long week.

I am not talking about white-guilt.

Working within urban settings and mission trips has helped me in this area. I am sure this is an effort that will take my entire life to truly "get."

## PORTAL TO HEAVEN

The disadvantage of being white with respect to understanding other cultures and races can turn into an advantage when it makes me deliberately have to stretch to touch the hand of Jesus who reached out to the different ethnicities of His day.

*Then the woman of Samaria said to Him, 'How is it that You, being a Jew, ask a drink from me, a Samaritan woman?' For Jews have no dealings with Samaritans.*

**John 4:9 (NKJV)**

I am white. I think I think "white."

One of the ways that this was pointed out to me was through a television interview with a young woman who was multiracial.

Asked about her mixed ethnicity and how it effects her viewpoint and life, she smiled without hesitation or one chip on her shoulder and answered: "I just can't wait until the time when most of the world will eventually be like me and then it won't matter anymore."

That stopped me in my tracks. Multiracial dating and eventual marriage and families are more common for a number of reasons. It's not just about war brides anymore. Ease of travel, the internet, educational visas and immigration have all helped many countries –not just America - become melting pots.

Pop culture, media, literature, careers and the world economy add to this palette for the impressionistic painting of the races.

## PORTAL TO HEAVEN

Recognize the speed in which multiculturalism is happening. The multiracial girl's observation leads us to see that Jesus is breaking barriers today with the same hand and timing that He did when He touched women, lepers, Samaritans, Canaanites and even enemy soldiers. Many of us are mutts in one way or another. We're from blended families, blended ethnicities or blended cultures. Being proud of being a pure-bred is breeding ground for pride. May it not cause anyone horror who reads this that there will probably come a time when "mixing it up a bit" won't be any harder than looking in a mirror.

*Then Peter replied, 'I see very clearly that God shows no favoritism.'*

**Acts 10:34 (NLT)**

"He's looks bizarre," I say…. "He's hip," you say.

One of the interesting things about traveling is that it unmasks petty preferences pretty rapidly. Idioms and accents, dress, boundaries, driving, grooming patterns and a host of other things we perceive as idiosyncratic mannerisms or abnormal behavior are quite normal in a place like, say northern Oregon, where the motto is "Keep Portland Weird." Weird gets wildly wider with the wind.

You have to admire people who very quickly slide into a new normal – and not just the Army brats in the hallways of their new high schools. These are the ones who immediately embrace something that's a little "different" as "interesting" without a hint of sarcasm in their euphemism versus those who would call that same thing "strange" with their nose either plugged or in the air.

The best missionaries, for example, are deftly cross-cultural and they accept norms that others would be frustrated by and/or think quite inferior to their idea of norm. Will missionaries then do better in heaven as well where the human race finally becomes one race after a terribly long race to get there?

## PORTAL TO HEAVEN

God deliberately helps us bump into other cultures in fast-food joints, work cubicles, public bathrooms and wherever. Beauty is in the eye of the beholder. May we get spiritual eyeglass prescriptions written with heaven's hand so we are no longer seeing "weird."

*Stop passing judgment on one another… Do not slander one another…Live in harmony with one another…Accept one another as Christ accepted you… In humility value others above yourselves…*

**Romans 14:13, James 4:11, Romans 12:16,**

**Romans 15:7, Phillipians 2:3. (All NIV)**

There was always plenty of chatter at our yacht club about Hell's Gate. Don't get to thinkin' that these guys are quoting scripture because that's not the nature of most boaters.

Actually, Hell's Gate is a narrow straight where the East River separating Manhattan from Long Island converges with water patterns from The Long Island Sound to create "strange tides." Some seriously dangerous rocks lie there like obstacles in a video game. Above all that, there is the lure of the lore. Boaters enjoy telling close-call stories the way fishermen throw lines about their catches.

Boaters in this area really can't avoid it as it's the E-Z Pass of the water. It's the plausible way to The Long Island Sound.

## PORTAL TO HEAVEN

We must go through some hell to get to where we are going.
We do not, however, have to do it alone. God has given believers
The Holy Spirit. Places like Hell's Gate are not where you
quote Henley's "Invictus:"
"It matters not how strait the gate, how charged with punishments the
scroll, I am the master of my fate: I am the captain of my soul."

At the risk of floating a watered down pun, no man is an island. Jesus
not only knows the water, He's walked on it and saved more than a
few overconfident seafarers who might be tempted to leave out His
assistance when reciting their tall tales of Hell's Gate.

*...the boat [was] beaten by the waves, for the wind was against them... But
immediately Jesus spoke to them, saying, 'Take heart; it is I. Do not be afraid...
In this world you will have trouble. But take heart! I have overcome the
world... We have this hope as an anchor for the soul...*

**Matthew 14:24, 27 (NIV), John 16:33 (NIV), Hebrews 6:19 (NIV)**

"Super Heroes" are as numerically advanced as Super Bowls...
"Batman 37 – The Saga Continues" isn't exactly a "Wham!" or "Bam!"
"Spiderman 23 – The Webmaster" employs the sticky star as a shy
IT guy.

Come on, now. Can I get a witness that Hollywood is often
creatively bankrupt and shamelessly borrows on past comic book
characters the way a still-at-home thirty-year-old hits up Grandpa
for some extra date money for cutting his hedges?

Actually, Hollywood knows what it's doing. It's good versus
evil and it doesn't need to be anything more than that. Why?

It's because we relate to the feeling of always being chased down
or rescued by something or someone determined to make our life
bad or good.

It could be an IRS worker, a mechanic or the ticket taker at the
Marvel 3-D Theatre who wants to hit us up for twenty bucks a seat.
Worse yet, it could be a doctor with a report that makes us feel like
we're in the movies. Simultaneously, it could be that grandpa who
simply wants to take us out for ice cream.

## ᴘORTAL ᴛO ʜEAVEN

The clarity with which entertainment mimics the gospel is incredible.
Today, there will be some good and some bad. They will intersect like
some of the collision-course car commercials. There will be conflicts
and cross-ups set against a beautiful sunset. There will be a really bad
sunburn on a stunning beach. We don't need to be in the movies as
this good-evil thing plays out all around us. Isn't that just Marvel-ous?
We don't need to be in the movies. It's all around. Well that's
just Marvel-ous.

*Yet man is born to trouble as surely as sparks fly upward.*

**Job 5:7, (NIV) [See Superhero Paul in 2 Corinthians 11:23ff]**

The consistent interplay of good and bad could cause schizophrenia if one is not careful. Every day, healing is juxtaposed with suffering. Just walk down some critical care units. One room has hopeful news for the patient while the very next room is enveloped in tragedy. One nurse is kind, one is im-patient.

In any given neighborhood, one person is getting a raise while another is facing cutbacks that swallow up a 22-year career.

I'm feeling good. But when I call you up, you can hardly get out of bed. And let's not even dive into the area of relationships. Can you spell, "Yo-Yo?"

As a writer, I am consistently trying to make sense of life's plot, draw out some sort of lesson and reason and have a safe landing when I finish the chapter. But the pen of life is not in my hands. It's as if there are seven billion pens are writing a seesaw novel or composing a dissonant symphony or the same number of brushes are painting on the one canvas.

## ⱣORTAL ⱭO ⱧEAVEN

For a novelist, The Garden of Eden made a lot of sense. With that kind of setting, a naked and passionate couple and The Gardener who tended to both, it would be easy to write that love story. It's not exactly an inside secret that novelists are forever searching for the words lost in that garden that are the missing pieces for the story's end. I draw my sanity and inspiration from The Novelist whose pen was dipped in blood.

*'It is finished,' He said.*

**Jesus, taken from the love story found in John 19:30 (NIV)**

It was a spectacular day. Eighty degrees and sunny. Fresh air.

What awaited me inside my office was even better. I walked into my hearing aid exam room and I got to witness a miracle of technology. Someone whose hearing loss previously made him check out of conversations and life could suddenly follow everything I was saying.

During this wondrous victory, a note was slid under my door explaining that the other practitioner and his office manager were going to a funeral. It turns out they had seen one of their patients just hours before he was crushed in a horrific work accident.

There is an ever-simultaneous juxtaposition of good and bad. I know about The Optimist club. Is there a "Reality Club" for people like me?

Woody Allen once said, "If one guy is starving somewhere, that puts a crimp on my evening." Well, Woody, you're going to have a lot of long nights.

"You gotta take the bad with the good" was how my parents phrased it. Learning that is like homework for the soul. Still, I don't think God ever intended me to hold my nose and gutsy my way through life.

## PORTAL TO HEAVEN

We experience pain alongside good. It makes us wondrously more mortal which makes us wondrously more immortal. Jesus was clothed in this same paradox and still had two feet on the ground.

*When the time came, he set aside the privileges of deity and took on the status of a slave, became human! Having become human, he stayed human...*

**Philippians 2:6 (The Message)**

Analogies may be both clear and ambiguous at the same time.

A good example of this is when we talk about the struggles of good and evil or whether life is blessed or hard, the comparison naturally drifts toward that of wartime.

But while that analogy is clear, is it accurate? Battles are usually fought by two armies of relatively equal power. If not, the lesser one should simply concede. When I regard Satan and his troops with equitable ability to God, I have bought into an analogy that's worse than ambiguity. It's an ambush.

There are blows and we could get mortally-wounded as this is indeed a fight. We can never underestimate the powers of hell. But analogies can actually produce mindsets that undermine reality.

A friend of mine wrote that her dad was a paratrooper in World War II during D-Day and said that the French were incredible people. Though their country was in ruins in The Spring, they were still planting gardens. That's a clearer analogy. The war certainly wasn't over and yet their faith produced a bumper crop of hope and confidence.

## PORTAL TO HEAVEN

Soldiers who have tasted war feel which direction the battle is going. Some have even sensed victory even while in the jaws of defeat because they found they were a handbreadth from their enemy's throat.

*And when the centurion, who stood there in front of Jesus, saw how he died, he said, 'Surely this man was the Son of God'... he disarmed the spiritual rulers and authorities. He shamed them publicly by his victory over them on the cross.*

**Mark 15:39 (NLT), Colossians 2:15 (NLT)**

(This Week's Portal will be on unity using the acronym of U.N.I.T.Y.)

U = Unified

"Tens of thousands of Christians will be gathered at Washington, D.C.'s National Mall…" No, they were not protesting. They were there to mark their solidarity for Jesus and the nation they love.

Differing theology, politics and social norms brushed together on the lawns around The Washington Monument.

From hearing the different speakers, musicians and the organizer of the event, one could postulate that there's a big chance that Christians are more united than they think. Attendees were of different color, from varying regions and came from rural and urban areas. Yet, they worshipped together. Some could poke holes in this theory by pointing to the disunity and segregation in Main Street churches.

Where I've been convicted lately is not in the area of unity, but in the aspect of being so sure that my opinions are those of God. I am not so sure anymore.

## ᏢORTAL ᏟᎢO ᎻEAVEN

The Washington rally made it clear that people see God differently than myself. I can look at hundreds of thousands of people on The Capitol Mall and reassure myself that they are all wrong or I can ask myself, "What am I missing?"

*Now John answered and said, 'Master, we saw someone casting out demons in Your name, and we forbade him because he does not follow with us.' But Jesus said to him, 'Do not forbid him, for he who is not against us is on our side.'*

**Luke 9:49,50 (NHEB). Editor's emphasis.**

"U.N.I.T.Y." N = Not Nationalism

Spiritual unity is not and will never be nationalism - not in America and not in any nation.

Pertaining to America, we are getting further and further away from any sense of the homogenous ideal that the country was founded upon: sacrifice and service. Think The American Revolution or World War II. At one time, there seemed to be a direct correlation between that kind of courage and goodness and America's prosperity.

America's apple pie has been divided into so many slices and there are so many cooks in the kitchen that they can't even agree that apples should supply the filling.

It's probably the logical extension of The Statue of Liberty's between-the-lines call for "the more the merrier." Eventually, the simmering philosophies and beliefs that led people to our shores melted the pot and it's now leaking into havoc. We claim to be "one nation under God." Now, we don't even agree on our God.

This may break a lot of nationalistic hearts. Take some solace from Israel who tried to make Christ an earthly king. They didn't understand his meaning of the "kingdom of God." Even if that had been based on nationalism, Israel would have to get their cues from The Bible. That didn't even work in their theocracy because of disobedience.

## PORTAL TO HEAVEN

There is a reason for the order of the saying, "For God and country."

*And I, when I am lifted up from the earth, will draw all people to myself.*

**John 12:32 (NIV)**

"U.N.I.T.Y." I = Individual

As much as the topic of "Unity" is a collective one, it rises and falls on the individual. There is the irony of how uniqueness forms unity and there is the horror of how individualism destroys all hope of such union.

How can such a vast universe of thought and matter ~~could~~ be entrusted to the sphere between our two ears. As I have aged, I trust that 6"X 6" space less and less. The 6"+ 6" below my brain is the safer place to land. Within that complex, says scripture, flow all of the issues of life.

Now that same book also says, "The heart is deceitful above all things and beyond cure. Who can understand it?" (Jeremiah 17:9 NIV) But turn the pages and a promise emerges: "I will give you a new heart and put a new spirit in you; I will remove from you your heart of stone and give you a heart of flesh." (Ezekiel 36:26)

So why the heart over the head? It really isn't a false dichotomy to phrase that question that way. I'm shifting toward the heart because my head peaks out about 5'8" above the ground whereas my heart can enjoy boundless heights.

## ₽ORTAL ꞆO ᖴEAVEN

We recognize that it is only when this hollow 6"x 6" space becomes holy that an individual can change into a saint who has "communion with God." That's the only true way to unity with people.

*Above all else, guard your heart, for everything you do flows from it.*

**Proverbs 4:23 (NIV)**

"U.N.I.T.Y." T = Together

Unity is a little hard from afar. How many "long-distance" romantic relationships have failed? There is something about time and space that makes unity tougher, despite "Facetime," "Skype" and other virtual tools.

It's the same thing with unity movements whether religious or political. Political conventions are awash with sound-bites and huggy photo-op attempts to project unity even when we know that the candidates were pummeling each other weeks ago.

A former boss insisted I see dissatisfied clientele in person because it's too easy to be curt over the phone. Yet, they would offer you a cup of coffee when you'd see them in person. It's like the etiquette of drivers who will rant at someone who cut them off, but would never act that way if they accidentally bumped into each other on a sidewalk.

A unity gathering I attended drew tens of thousands of Christians to Washington, D.C. with the kind of diversity you'd expect at a ballpark. Despite sweltering temperatures, they focused on worship, prayer, teaching and exhortation.

## PORTAL TO HEAVEN

The Washington gathering put us together like sardines in a can. Our cooler bumped up against another cooler and our blanket was alongside the Midwest couple with all the squirmy kids and our voices were blending with those who worshiped in broken English. For one day, we were literal neighbors and close ones at that. It raises the question: "What if the church regularly, deliberately and uncomfortably cross-pollinated in every city and town?"

*When they heard this sound, a crowd came together in bewilderment, because each one heard their own language being spoken.*

**Acts 2:6 (NIV)**

"U.N.I.T.Y." Y = You

God brings people and churches from all over the globe into his "laboratory of love." Like every experiment of matter where one thing is built upon another and there is some nucleus, so it is with the bonding of people.

The experiment can't start at its end. We can't expect to bring several facets of the church or the nation or even an organization together and by their mere existence in the same building expect that the bonds of unity would fall into place.

That would be like taking all of the ingredients, test animals and tubes and laying them on the lab counter and somehow hope that the experiment will take care of itself.

With His lab coat on, we see that God's research is impeccable and the process is well underway. He builds from the nucleus as said in Ephesians 4:2-4 (BSB) "…with all humility and gentleness, with patience, bearing with one another in love, and with diligence to preserve the unity of the Spirit through the bond of peace. There is one body and one Spirit, just as you were called to one hope…"

## PORTAL TO HEAVEN

We must see the part "You" play in this lavish love lab. This scripture points to "You," which includes "Me." The only time the "Genesis Experiment" blows up in the lab is when we don't humble ourselves and cooperate so The Great Scientist can finally complete His work.

*I pray not only for these, but also for those who believe in Me through their message. May they all be one, as You, Father, are in Me and I am in You. May they also be one in Us, so the world may believe You sent Me.*

**John 17:20, 21 (HCSB)**

- 228 -

How many times in one extended weekend can you watch the Independence Day fireworks and not be in danger of taking them for granted? Four days before the Fourth, there were simultaneously four fireworks celebrations visible from our bedroom window. While some were grander than others, it felt as though they were choreographed due to their varying distances.

On the following night, a free "Classical Concert on the Waterfront" featured engaging selections and a finale of Americana classics and marches that were accented by a full-scale fireworks assault the likes The Continental Army had not witnessed. However, within minutes, spectators were picking up their lawn chairs – barely noticing the display.

It was also announced that this concert series is a traveling show and each concert will be followed by… you guessed it: fireworks.

The city's baseball team is playing on The Fourth of July. Root, oh root for the home team. If they don't win, it won't be a shame because the game will climax with fireworks.

## PORTAL TO HEAVEN

Too much of anything might offer an invitation to indifference as was witnessed at the waterfront concert and fireworks display where only some put their hands over their hearts during The National Anthem. The rest failed to notice the bombs bursting in air.

*If you find honey, eat just enough– too much of it, and you will vomit…*
*'But they paid no attention and went their way, one to his own farm,*
*another to his business.'*

**Proverbs 25:16 (NIV), Matthew 22:5 (NASB)**

Although over 11,000 amendments to the Constitution have been proposed, none of the original ten that were passed have ever been repealed directly or indirectly. The first successful amendments are called "The Bill of Rights" and were protections added on, or amended, to The Constitution. Their general purpose is to keep individual liberties intact.

Having traveled throughout countries where poverty, discrimination and religious repression are rampant, I can only come to one conclusion: the governments and their laws don't have the same commitment to individual liberty *from* their own government that we do.

How we accomplish such protections and philosophy is through a deliberate checks-and-balance government – a foresight built on the premise of the distrust of the human heart once it has acquired power.

Remembering England's grip, it is good to remember that we cherish our liberties from our own government and its unreasonable reach into the individual. For the faith-filled Christian, it is no small thing to practice our faith personally and in any and all form of assembly.

## PORTAL TO HEAVEN

There is irony that righteous laws induce freedom. They reflect a higher law; ones that were based on God's Ten Commandments. Those who choose without compulsion to obey these laws will find themselves free from the tyranny of their own heart – a wretched monarchy ruled by hell itself.

*Do we, then, nullify the law by this faith? Not at all! Rather, we uphold the law.*

**Romans 3:31 (NIV)**

It's not Disney World. It just seems that way.

Meticulously-landscaped yards introduce a passerby to 20-room Victorians just a few feet from century-old sidewalks that are under a canopy of trees lining the perfectly laid-out streets. The wrap-around porches are shaded by traditional canvas awnings. Step back and take a photo. Your shot could make it into *Better Homes & Gardens*.

One might wonder if you could make the argument that Spring Lake, New Jersey is what Jesus had in mind when he talked about his Father having "many mansions." The idyllic town is called the "Irish Rivieria." Located on the Jersey shore just an hour train-ride away from Manhattan, it is not hard to guess where the wealth originates.

It's Rockwell on steroids. It's a summer paradise. Walk to the beach. Bike to a Main Street that Rockwell somehow missed. There, sheik boutiques, a deli famous for pork roll and cheese breakfast sandwiches and an American Flag as big as the sky all wave at the tourists.

There's only thing the mansions are missing: people. Usually, most of the porches are empty. No badminton in the yard. No croquet. Maybe the wealthy needed to get away from tourists like me so they went off to the *other* Riviera.

## ꝑORTAL ꝿO ꞕEAVEN

Taking things for granted is not something reserved for the rich and famous. Wherever we are, might it not be nice to invite a loved or lonely one over for a spot of tea on our own porch?

*On a good day, enjoy yourself; On a bad day, examine your conscience. God arranges for both kinds of days so that we won't take anything for granted.*

**Ecclesiastes 7:14 (The Message)**

Out of all of the things we could be in danger of taking for granted, relationships should be at the top of the list. We should regularly ask ourselves: "Are there any friends or relatives that I assume will always be there?"

That one question might reveal something that none of us want to examine.

In any given relationship, one will die before the other. If I go first, do I really want to go to the grave with a flippant or unintentional heart toward that person? If he or she dies first, do I want to walk into his or her wake carrying the weight of a sloppily-handled relationship?

Naturally, people move in and out of our lives. Relocation, job changes and even attending a different house of faith can all inadvertently affect relationships.

Not to scare anyone, but some unexpected move, change of circumstance or even death could be closer than any of us would like to imagine. This shouldn't cause fear and anxiety. It is simply true.

How might we approach relationships differently with this in mind?

## PORTAL TO HEAVEN

The Almighty will bring people home at His appointed time. And if God gives and God takes away, then we should be circumspect about what He has given now rather than blame Him when they are taken away.

*You saw me before I was born. Every day of my life was recorded in your book. Every moment was laid out before a single day had passed... So you, too, must keep watch! For you do not know the day or hour of my return.*

**Psalm 139:16 (NLT), Matthew 25:13 (NLT)**

It might seem unthinkable to take God for granted. Really, He ain't going anywhere. But would we treat our spouse or best friend in such manner?

My adopted father told me that we are in the greatest danger of complacency and/or pride when things are going well.

You don't have to be a biblical scholar to note that Old Testament Israel got into trouble when the land was flowing with milk and honey. As livestock, employees, and tents increased, the people forgot who gave them their fortunes.

Flash forwarding, America has in many ways become the wealthiest and most advanced culture in history.

There is much evidence that we have taken God for granted. Abandoned and dying churches litter the landscape. Church attendance and decaying steeples aren't the only clues. Every technological device is capable of providing evidence that can indict America (and other countries) of her spiritual slide. We don't think about it because we've gotten used to the blasphemy, vulgarity and immorality.

There are many reasons for taking God for granted beyond prosperity. Good health, numerous relationships and simply getting caught up with ourselves can all add to the list.

## PORTAL TO HEAVEN

We hate being taken for granted by those we deeply love. If we are made in God's image, from whom do you think we got that trait?

*In all your ways acknowledge him… So, because you are lukewarm–neither hot nor cold–I am about to spit you out of my mouth. You say, 'I am rich… you do not realize that you are wretched, pitiful, poor, blind and naked.'*

**Pr. 3:6 (ESV), Rev. 3:16,17 (NIV)**

I have obsessive tendencies when it comes to sunrises. I bought a house that faces the east so that I could witness the yellow ball start his circuit every morning. I have been known to drive miles and miles to catch that sunrise over the ocean.

This obsession is probably heaven's trick on me because God knows that I'm more than a bit sluggish in the morning and coffee alone just doesn't cut it. So, God arranged something that captures my attention: beauty.

First, the pre-dawn sky is sheer, stunning beauty -just the opposite of "It's darkest before dawn." The actual sunrise usually pales to the opening act. So, what would instigate the shaking off of slumber more than beauty? Very cunning, God.

If beauty is in the eye of the beholder, what do I see?

As at an art gallery, I see The Artist's heart on display. I happen to love the color purple. He usually splashes some of that on the canvas of the sky. Then, there's the "live" canvas aspect. Like staring at a painting-in-the-making and seeing more and more within it, the sunrise is a continuum of colorful creativity. It's like a song that has a multitude of crescendos.

## ρORTAL ᴄTO ℲEAVEN

Every sunrise expresses the mastery of The Master. I am undone. Sometimes I wish I could capture it in a picture. It's never as good as the experience. The photo can only be representative of what is happening before my eyes.

Call my sunrise fascination an obsession. I call it beauty.

*God has made a home in the heavens for the sun. It bursts forth like a radiant bridegroom after his wedding. It rejoices like a great athlete eager to run the race.*

**Psalm 19:4,5 ((NLT)**

Sunrises capture the concept of second chances. No matter how bad the previous day, month or year, there's always this empty canvas before us.

Defeatism can sneak in at the end of a literal or figurative " day." It is at those times that we are the most susceptible to the attacks of Satan – usually in some form of condemnation.

"You really blew that today," the devil chides. "You wasted a lot of time today. You shouldn't have spent that money today. You didn't get your exercise today. You missed your devotional time today." All of these types of haunting reminders – for some or all could be true – are best leveled during our lowest times of resistance: the evening of a literal or figurative *day*.

When the sunrise comes, it's a metaphor of the second chance. It's as if the slate is completely clean.

Could it be that God knew we would know our failures so intimately in an internal fashion that He designed an external sign so audacious that it would make the Los Vegas strip like a nearly burned-out match? The angle of a sunrise makes it tough to look into without shielding your eyes. Clue here?

## ᏢORTAL ᏅTO ᏂEAVEN

The sunrise's recurring timing and brilliance is no accident. The sun and The Son daily burn away the mist of our failures. They silence the accusing devil – the same one who so vividly remembers another sunrise on the first Easter morning. It makes you want to say, "Touché" over and over and over again.

*When He [Jesus] had disarmed the rulers and authorities, He made a public display of them, having triumphed over them through.*

**Colossians 2:15 (NASB), Editor's brackets.**

Sunrises make us feel as if we've been given an exceptional allowance by Daddy…and we're sure looking forward to spending it!

Dad says we should spend it wisely, but He never said that we can't enjoy all of the time, talents and resources that He's generously given to us.

In terms of time, we should look at a sunrise in the way we look at a stopwatch. There is a deadline and the sunset will be here before we know it. It's only right to mix Holy Spirit-planning with Holy-Spirit leading. It's been said that time is an embezzler rather than a hold-up thief. It subtly brings us to the end of a day or a life.

With respect to our talents, it is so easy to "spend" our talents on ourselves. The skill-set tucked inside of us is unique. It's such a gift that to squander it during our day(s) would be an incalculable travesty.

And when it comes to resources, these are simply tools to build the kingdom of God. Each day, there is an expenditure on our part. The question is: Was that expenditure authorized?

When we were children, allowances brought up a lot of warm fuzzies about the goodness and generosity of our parents.

## PORTAL TO HEAVEN

The allowance that the sunrise allows reminds us like clockwork of the goodness of God and steers the day's expenditure in the right direction.

*…if you do not wake up, I will come like a thief… As long as it is day, we must do the works of him who sent me. Night is coming, when no one can work.*

**Revelation 3:3 (NASB), John 9:4 (NIV)**

Anyone who has had a sleepless night can attest that the evening's time is then exaggerated. Clock-watching only exacerbates the problem. And so this awful slowness turns into a nightmarish existence.

Besides the loss of sleep that portends a long and weary day, there is also a sense of loneliness that comes with counting sheep. There is really no one to call unless you resort to the advice of that cute wall plaque: "Before you go to sleep, give God all of your problems. He'll be up all night anyway." But that's reserved for those who can fall asleep.

Life has stretches of darkness when there really is no rest. That can happen through literal sleeplessness caused by physical or emotional pain or excessive worry. It can metaphorically happen over weeks, months and even years. This is why we call them "dark times."

Sometimes, darkness comes over us in the form of depression; a sense of uneasiness that can last for what seems to be forever.

A common form of utter darkness is sin. If allowed to go on unattended for years or a lifetime, a person will creep through a night that never ends on earth and will never end in eternity.

## PORTAL TO HEAVEN

Jesus is the light of the world. He brings the sunrise to all of the deep-night experiences of our lives. He is salvation for the sinner. He is the dawn for the sleepless. He is the "Sonrise of Our Souls."

*Arise, shine, for your light has come, and the glory of the LORD rises upon you...In Him was life, and the life was the light of men. And the light shines in the darkness...*

**Isaiah 60:1 (NIV), John 1:4 (NKJV)**

How did God arrange sunrises to take place in every time zone and from every spot on the earth?

Even seasons aren't as clear a metaphor for God's control over the earth because many regions don't have a lot of clear-cut seasons. But the sunrise is a different story.

And why did He weave the sunrise into the most glorious story of all time? Easter sunrise services - no matter how wakeful or sleepy they are – can never replicate the experience that Mary and the disciples had at the tomb.

Jesus' resurrection from the dead was so unthinkable and so out-of-the-box that Mary couldn't recognize Jesus when He was right next to her. She even volunteers to go get his body so that she could give him a proper burial.

She gets a pass for her error because a resurrection would have seemed bizarre. But we have no such excuse. Even with all we know about Easter and all of the theology surrounding it, we still seek to bury Jesus through worry, self-condemnation, unbelief, self-glorification, denial of sin and so on and so forth.

## ₽ORTAL ₲TO ℋEAVEN

God has given us the sunrise every morning and everywhere to remind us of the most unfathomable concept in the world: we can rise out of sin into a new life and an everlasting resurrection. There is a reason he is called "The Son."

*The steadfast love of the Lord never ceases; his mercies never come to an end; they are new every morning; great is your faithfulness.*

**Lamentations 3:22,23 (ESV)**

# September
## PORTALS TO HEAVEN

My work with seniors has taught me a few lessons about time and the big one is the cliché, "Time flies." Every elder I know has quoted that one to me, followed by a slight wink and the postscript, "You'll see."

I'm beginning to see.

However, my schedule recently slowed down like a flight layover at an airport where you don't have to switch planes. It's just long enough to regroup, but not long enough to get too comfortable. This opening in my schedule happened to be on September 22. My mom's literal portal to heaven took place on that day when she took flight to see her savior.

Since my calendar slowed down, I did too. I decided to walk around a graveyard. My mom and dad are buried three hours away, so I went to the cemetery where my adopted Dad and Mom were laid to rest.

I have a great attraction to cemeteries. Tranquility resurrects the dead...my deadness, in particular.

What is it about missing these people so deeply that it lands us where they now reside? Was it their kindness? Was it the manner in which God placed them in our lives where we lived and not positioned them 8,000 miles away in another culture or land where we would have never met?

## PORTAL TO HEAVEN

Although the dead cannot be replaced, they have sown into us the part of them we miss so much. So if you see a reflection in their tombstone...

*Consider others as more important than yourselves.*

**Philippians 2:3 (HCSB)**

Portals to heaven can be literal and that is exactly the situation when a loved one dies.

When death takes someone near to them, the atheist, agnostic and believer alike wonder about the concept within this scripture: "Your eyes have seen my unformed substance; and in Your book were all written the days that were ordained for me, when as yet there was not one of them." (Psalm 139:16)

Internally, most of us think about when our ticket will be punched. But rather than interpret this passage in light of our final passage, perhaps it would be good to look at those who have made the trip and think about how they spent each day in "the days that were ordained."

My first authentic prayer partner was an older woman. Her days were filled with prayer and she was always thinking about others. I distinctly remember being next to her in prayer. I felt that we were standing next to God. It was that intimate. That's how she spent her days.

## ᏢORTAL ᏆO ᎻEAVEN

As I think about the days ordained for me, I don't want to get too far ahead of myself by thinking of the day of my "passage." It's better to think on this day instead of that day by meditating on these words:

*One thing I ask from the Lord, this only do I seek: that I may dwell in the house of the Lord <u>all the days of my life,</u> to gaze on the beauty of the Lord and to seek him in his temple.*

**Psalm 27:4 (NIV) Editor's emphasis.**

## Premature Passages (Part 1)

Rich Mullins was one of my favorite songwriters of all time. The guy who penned "Awesome God" and countless classics was also a gifted musician. At 41, this genius died in an auto accident. At the time, he was working on *The Jesus Record* that he said was his most important musical work to date.

Most of his fans, including me, would say they had portals of heaven through his poignant and honest lyrics that were birthed from a tortured soul of sorts.

More than a tad maverick, he described himself as an "equal opportunity offender" with regard to his convicting concerts and dialogues. He carried around his guitar and his hurt. His "father wound" played itself out in alcohol, identity issues, insecurity and loneliness as a single man. But his wounds also added rich and raw texture to his ballads and pop hits.

## PORTAL TO HEAVEN

Rich Mullins will be remembered for the portals to heaven of his life just as much as his music. He was the successful gold-album Christian artist who ditched Nashville and asked his accountant to pay him only what the average U.S. worker made and then spent his days teaching on a Navajo reservation. Fittingly, he became interested in the poverty of Jesus as expressed through St. Francis – both of whom had "premature passages" in some eyes.

*But when I leave I want to go out like Elijah. With a whirlwind to fuel my chariot of fire. And when I look back on the stars, it'll be like a candlelight in central park and it won't break my heart to say goodbye. By Rich Mullins. For we know that when this earthly tent we live in is taken down…we will have a house in heaven, an eternal body made for us by God himself…*

**2 Corinthians 5:1 (NLT)**

## Premature Passages (Part II)

Sometimes portals to heaven can be through a "premature" death. "Cut short" is the term we use to describe a tragedy of this sort.

Dirk was a treasured friend that I had just begun discipling when a horrible car accident took his life. It didn't make much sense. He had embraced Jesus as his Savior and he turned from depending on drugs to truly living out the gospel on a daily basis. He once gave away his nice coat to a street person. He would spend time at the community college witnessing to students about the miraculous change in his life. And his bright blue eyes shone with the love of Christ to the point that I wondered who was mentoring who.

To help me deal with his sudden death, I wrote a song that included the line, "Clocks can't tell the time."

## PORTAL TO HEAVEN

When a short burst of Christ-like love meets our intellect, we'd be better off to look at their portals to heaven rather than correct God about His timing. Satan seeks to rob, kill and destroy. Suicides, violence and accidents can be used by the enemy. I cannot claim to be an expert on premature deaths. But Dirk's "short" life gave me some very clear portals to heaven that are still with me - that's the LONG and short of it.

*...making the very most of your time [on earth, recognizing and taking advantage of each opportunity and using it with wisdom and diligence], because the days are [filled with] evil.*

**Ephesians 5:16 (Amplified Bible)**

The last conversation I had with my dad was about God. He had some buried hurt about the church he attended. Uh, does that sound familiar to anyone???

Dad was a plumbing contractor and the church evidently gave some work he had bid on to a company whose owner was of a different faith. It pinched him very badly. I am positive the church leaders and building committee had no idea how much that affected his outlook on God. Perhaps there was a good reason for their decision, but it obviously wasn't explained enough to massage Dad's hurt feelings.

Years later, my final conversation with Dad was about God – not contracts. Yet, that simple snub was enough for him to somehow substitute the "church" with "God."

While petty conflicts can trip up almost anyone, this conversation with my dad stopped me in my tracks. I am an ambassador of Christ and God can use me in this fashion to represent Him and become another's portal to heaven. That's quite a responsibility.

When I hurt another and think it's petty, I may have just plugged their portal to heaven. It's not up to me to decide what should be important to another. (I am not talking about confronting someone on sin and/or salvation.)

## PORTAL TO HEAVEN

God gives little you and me this gigantic job of helping people see heaven clearly; not fuzzy. I can't rationalize away that the other person is being "petty."

*If possible, so far as it depends on you, be at peace with all men...*
*Paul the Apostle, who knew first hand the results of infighting -*

**Romans 12:18 (NAS)**

I know we should not text and drive. But what about seeing Portals of Heaven while I'm behind the wheel?

It happens all of the time. Cars have a way of enclosing us like a child who is in a safety seat so we'd better roll with it.

I have a lifelong tendency to cut it close when it comes to my schedule. This leads to being a classic "10-Over" (the speed limit). This leads to a recurring scene in my life: I can read the fine print on the bumper sticker ahead of me. I'm not proud of hugging someone's tail. But there I am, always gripping the wheel, craning my neck out the window in search of my salvation through the dotted lines that will allow me to get the heck ahead of this deadbeat driver.

Through the mercy of God, these slow drivers have saved me dozens of potential "speed-trap" tickets.

It's reminiscent of times when I wanted God to move a little faster in my life and there were slowpokes or obstacles in my way. It led to frustration, impatience and anger. But God's slowness never did me any harm.

If God had given me my way, He would have had to write me a ticket of discipline just up the road of life that would have been analogous to losing my license.

## ᑭORTAL ᑕᎢO ᎻEAVEN

Some may say that it's good to walk ever-so-slightly behind Jesus.
That's a little different from hugging God's tail.

*So Sarai said to Abram, 'Now behold, the LORD has prevented me from bearing children. Please go in to my maid; perhaps I will obtain children through her.' And Abram listened to the voice of Sarai.*

**Genesis 16:2 (NASB)**

"Sunday driver!"

That used to be the common derogatory term for slow drivers.

I knew a few. I would group them as, "Seniors, Texters & My Mom (maybe yours, as well)."

For example, Mom was a fairly cautious driver. Who could blame her with seven kids in the car? Naturally, other drivers were probably a bit perturbed by her anticipation of that yellow light.

And then there's the hunched-over senior citizen with extremely thick glasses who is plodding along in front of me. She's so short that it looks like no one is in the driver seat.

Oh, and we can't forget the texter who is sitting at the light ten minutes after it turns green.

As for following funeral processions and school buses, I suppose they get a pass...but just barely.

I am a notorious "Jersey-Driver" by birth and preference.

Recently, I was back in my home state driving my old four-cylinder Honda CRV. A Mercedes E-Class and a Maserati were weaving in and out of the heavy Jersey shore traffic and came right up on my bumper. Guess who was the pokey-man then?

## PORTAL TO HEAVEN

Slow drivers have actually become a recurring (ugh) portal to heaven to me. Driving is communal – just like relationships. If I get this impatient with slow drivers, what am I doing with people who don't move as fast as I do in life?

*Don't push your way to the front; don't sweet-talk your way to the top. Put yourself aside, and help others get ahead.*

**Philippians 2:3 (The Message)**

**Wife:** "I think traffic laws are there for our protection and that stop lights keep us safe."

**Husband:** "I think red lights are of Satan. If I could, I would drive on the sidewalks to avoid them."

I hate to say it but I'm with the husband. Does that make me an official citizen of Italy?

If I had my way, we'd build circles and bridges at every corner, "No Right on Red" would be outlawed, left-arrow lights would be required, middle turning lanes would be free game, tickets would be written for those who slowed down at traffic circles or exiled to India until they learn that beeping beats braking and America would consume infinitely less gas from idling at those satanic red lights.

I grew up in New Jersey and actually loved competing with Manhattan's cabbies for that coveted green light or one-way turn. Seriously, I am not reckless nor do I advocate a disregard for the law. I've been blessed with good motoring skills, reflexes, lots of mileage behind the wheel and very low insurance rates as a result of a safe driving record. I also know my limits and the overall design of the roads by engineers and a little about Mother Nature's role.

## ℘ORTAL ℧O ℍEAVEN

Laws and design are for everyone's safety and their constraints are analogous to spiritual laws and designs. There actually are state police officers and traffic engineers in heaven – even though I didn't think so while growing up in New Jersey.

*For rulers hold no terror for those who do right, but for those who do wrong. Do you want to be free from fear of the one in authority? Then do what is right and you will be commended.*

**Romans 13:3 (NIV)**

I have joined the rest of the human race in caving in to the *Global Positioning Systems (GPS)* while going to a destination that I had formerly driven to by memory. It's like phone numbers. I don't or can't memorize them anymore.

My wife and I can actually have three distinct routes generated at once between the car's dashboard, her phone and my phone. You can imagine the clash when all three are simultaneously saying, "Turn right," "Turn Left" and "Proceed." So far, these GPS units have not started arguing with each other over whose route is the best. I'll leave that to some sci-fi writer.

There was a time when I resisted trusting some satellite instead of my instincts. And yet, I am now lazy when it comes to digging into my memory and creative nature in figuring out the best route on my own. I wonder how long it will take me to cave in to the self-driving cars.

## ᑭORTAL ᑕTO ᕼEAVEN

A lazy reliance on GPS is analogous to our devotional lives or private lives with God. For example, instead of keeping scripture verses tucked into our hearts and journaling and talking with God, we can be tempted to rely on the latest devotional book, podcast, app, radio or TV program that steers us rather than getting direction from The Lord. *God's Positioning System* is a combination of keeping our eyes on God's Word, relishing His hand in ours and not being afraid to make a wrong turn.

*...let God transform you into a new person by changing the way you think. Then you will learn to know God's will for you, which is good and pleasing and perfect... Seek the Kingdom of God above all else, and live righteously, and he will give you everything you need.*

**Romans 12:2 (NLT), Matthew 6:33 (NLT)**

Driving has a way of teaching me life lessons because the solitude seems to be a great place to listen to the wheels spinning…in my head.

For example, I have often wondered what drives me to drive fast. I know that poor planning, procrastination and losing track of time can independently or combine to make me run behind schedule.

But I always knew beneath the hood of my brain, the cylinders weren't hitting just right. This led me to bluntly ask God, "What drives me so hard?"

If it was simply a holy passion, even a hypersensitive one, I could just ease up on the accelerator and enjoy the ride a bit more. After all, I can admire the horsepower of John Wesley's engine who galloped over 250,000 miles so his master could preach in as many towns as possible. It's not that simple and I ain't no John Wesley.

I didn't ask Siri. I asked God who pointed out that some of my pedal-to-the-medal stuff was validation-oriented and a misinterpretation of the motivations of Jesus and all the Wesleys of the world.

## PORTAL TO HEAVEN

In the not-so-quiet of my car, there has been a gradual release of the wheel to The Holy Spirit. He keeps pointing to Jesus who, though driven to serve His Dad, was never given a speeding ticket.

*But Jesus said to them, 'My Father never stops working, and so I keep working, too'… Jesus traveled through all the towns and villages of that area, teaching in the synagogues and announcing the Good News about the Kingdom…*
*And what do you benefit if you gain the whole world but lose your own soul?*

**John 5:17 (NCV), Matthew 9:35 (NLT), Mark 8:36 (NLT)**

The Morning Star (Venus) invites itself into our bedroom, nudges me to wake up and then returns to its place outside my window that looks close enough to touch but as far away as heaven itself.

In his masterful, *100 Portraits of Christ*, author Henry Gariepy finishes his volume by painting Jesus as "The Bright Morning Star."

According to Gariepy, Jesus split eternity into two. I can see this represented before dawn as the morning star cuts evening off from the morning. (Interestingly, it is seen as the evening star as well.)

When The Morning Star refuses to subside even in the "darkest before dawn" scenario, I see how the crucifixion portends the resurrection. When the Morning Star contrasts with the pitch-black night outside my window, I am reassured that there is light at the end of any tunnel. These tunnels are a bit more haunting when it's 3 or 4 in the morning. Yet, what victory resides in such utter blackness as this truism arises as surely as the sun: darkness can never extinguish the light.

## ᑭORTAL ᒍTO ᕼEAVEN

Whatever circumstance or emotion is presenting itself in my life, I look to Jesus' death. Somehow, he died and then lived through the tomb. Some theologians explain that Christ was busy amassing souls from hell during that time. Whatever exactly occurred, I am acutely aware that Jesus does raise me from whatever dark spell I am currently under and I am ever thankful for the nudge each dawn by The Morning Star.

*I will give him the morning star…I, Jesus…I am the Bright and Morning Star.*

**Revelation 2:28 (ESV), 22:16 (NLT)**

I went to bed with a lot on my mind and a lot on my plate. So, something tangible, certain and close, would be nice.

I had been getting up rather early and this flashlight in the sky called The Morning Star kept getting my notice. But on this particular night, there were stars in a row above it that led straight to the moon. So, that's where the expression about stars "lining up" originated.

I can't say that I jumped out of bed and everything turned out right. I can't even say I really believe that a line in the sky means things will go fine or get better. But I suddenly understood how someone came up with that adage in light of the perfection of my Maker. You have to consider these stars are light years away and yet on this night they could pass for a yardstick. How is that possible?

## ᖹORTAL ᑐO ᖷEAVEN

This literal portal seemed as clear as a teacher's theorem on the chalkboard – to the teacher, that is. Even though I didn't go back to sleep, I rested easier. You don't have to be one of the three wise men to realize that God really is in control – even when you are waking up at what some call "ungodly hours."

*Your lovingkindness, O LORD, extends to the heavens, Your faithfulness reaches to the skies.*

**Psalm 36:5 (NAS)**

The Morning Star is the brilliant light above the horizon that signals dawn's sure arrival. It is interesting that it appears during the darkest part of the night.

I don't know whether I can tell whether 2:30 a.m. is blacker than 3:30 a.m. But the expression, "It's darkest before dawn," may not have to do with a literal lack of light so much as it is the longest part of the night. Time-wise, it's the furthest point from the last time we saw light.

People who can't sleep, those that work the graveyard shift or even those caught camping in a tent on a chilly night can tell you that the pre-dawn sky seems like it will never change; the night feels as if it will go on forever.

This explains why The Morning Star is so welcome.

John Wycliffe, a pre-reformation priest and English scholar at Oxford, was known as "The Morning Star of the Reformation." His concern for church government and clergy corruption, the disadvantaged and the twisting and ignorance of the sacred Word of God brought him fame and scorn.

## PORTAL TO HEAVEN

The Morning Star cuts two ways: our spiritual-early-morning grogginess could tragically lead to missing moves of God that were His "morning star." But God could also use you and me to usher in something that the church is not quite ready for. Either way, let's get out of bed.

*But everything exposed by the light becomes visible—and everything that is illuminated becomes a light. This is why it is said: 'Wake up, sleeper, rise from the dead, and Christ will shine on you.' Be very careful, then, how you live— not as unwise but as wise, making the most of every opportunity, because the days are evil.*

**Ephesians 5:13-16 (NIV)**

Theologians talk about the "silent years" between The Old Testament and The New Testament. Could these have been the darkest times for Israel and, logically, for the world? If God doesn't speak, what hope can be drawn?

Perhaps this is why the wise men were looking at stars. Maybe this is why Simeon was waiting for the "consolation" of his people while Anna was aching for the "redemption" of the same. It could explain the fuss around the birth of the ministry of Jesus, with everyone asking, "Could this be the one?"

When things grow silent and dark and the only stirring is the light of the human soul affixed to the hope of the eternal, we understand the longing of all these great biblical figures. It is here that we understand that The Star of Bethlehem is, in fact, The Morning Star of eternity.

## ᛕORTAL ᛏO ᚺEAVEN

Darkness and hope are inextricably linked and there is a reason God gives us The Morning Star when it is not yet morning.

*We also have the prophetic message as something completely reliable, and you will do well to pay attention to it, as to a light shining in a dark place, until the day dawns and the morning star rises in your hearts.*

**2 Peter 1:19 (NIV)**

Like everyone else, I have heard over the last four decades that the return of Christ is imminent. From *The Late Great Planet Earth* through the Left Behind series to *Four Blood Moons*, I have moved from the edge of my seat to wondering if God was constructing a deeper chair for me.

I still believe we are in some sort of end-times scenario. I have no idea whether it's one year away or one century away. While I'm no Johnny Appleseed, I concur with Martin Luther who said, "If I knew that tomorrow was the end of the world, I would plant an apple tree today!"

The essential "positive" requirement for Jesus' return is that the gospel will be preached to all nations - now possible with media, missions and, of course, God's timing. Certainly, The Bride (God's church) will have to be ready.

What are the "negative" evidences that we are in final-curtain times? The darkness. It's the pitch-black tenor of our time. Of course, most will argue that evil, complaints about the younger generation and lack of civility have plagued humanity for centuries. But it is obvious that wickedness abounds.

## ꝒORTAL ꟲTO ꟼEAVEN

The darkest-before-dawn scenario points to The Morning Star's rising for the second time. Here comes The Son and I don't just say, "It's alright." I say, "Maranatha."

*...in the last days, perilous times will come: For men will be lovers of themselves, lovers of money, boasters, proud, blasphemers, disobedient to parents, unthankful, unholy, unloving, unforgiving, slanderers, without self-control, brutal, despisers of good, traitors, headstrong, haughty, lovers of pleasure rather than lovers of God, having a form of godliness but denying its powers.*

**2 Timothy 3:2-5 (NAS)**

Setbacks and even failures can still be used as ingredients in the stew of God and in the timing of when that concoction of particulars in our lives will be ready to serve.

For example, I distinctly remember my most un-favorite boss (as polite a euphemism as I could come up with). He handed me a box on a Friday and told me to pack up and leave.

I had seen these scenes in movies and always thought them a bit melodramatic. But here I found myself calling my wife for a ride home in the middle of the day.

Sheepishly, I exited the office in front of coworkers and shamefully got into the car with my wife and kids as an unemployed husband and father. No severance. No prospects - for I had not been looking. And there was not an ounce of self-esteem in my being.

It's easy to look back and talk of the comeback. But going through it was hell.

I received a call from my former boss who was the polar opposite of my un-favorite and she offered me a temporary job that was indirectly used by God to catapult me into a three-decade career that enabled me to help thousands of senior citizens.

## ᑭORTAL ᑕᎢO ᕼEAVEN

The best Chef in the world "creatively" used the broken pieces of my career to feed others with a tasty stew just when I thought my goose was cooked.

*And we know that in all things God works for the good of those who love him, who have been called according to his purpose.*

**Romans 8:28 (NIV)**

"Don't give up," Coach Lester said. "We still have one more inning."

But when your bats are silent through a whole game, an inning portended another donut.

I learned a big lesson that day as an 11 year-old who had never been on a championship team. When you haven't won, you don't know what winning is like. Usually, it requires some grit. Then there's the overcoming part. And almost always, it demands a comeback. That's why the best movies move the protagonist squarely up against a wall before he or she digs down and pulls out enough strength to come back.

But I hadn't been an overcomer yet. Coach Lester had. In Little League, the seventh inning is the final one and we were down to our last at-bat. I can't remember whether it was 1-0 or 0-0. That's when a big kid named Bill Majeski took a big swing and clobbered a home run. We went wild. We found out about "the comeback."

Coach Lester reminded us, "See, I told you not to give up."

## ᏢORTAL ᏠTO ᎱEAVEN

Belief, whether in baseball or faith, is seeing something that hasn't occurred yet. It was to be my only Little League championship. But I finally understood the vocabulary of Coach Lester. That language was to be necessary throughout my life.

*For a righteous man falls seven times, and rises again…*

**Proverbs 24:16 (NASB)**

Sports has great impact. It's the story. The underdog. The champion. And the comeback.

Being a Mets fan is an exercise in looking up…from the bottom of the food chain because we lived in the shadow of the giant Yankees. We don't have many glory-moments in our lifetime. Then came 1986…

The Mets were about to lose The World Series against The Boston Red Sox. The television screen began rolling the cost of a loaf of bread and the price of a house in 1918 - the last time The Red Sox won The World Series. For some reason –although depressed- I wouldn't get up from the couch until it was all over.

Boston was up by two runs in the bottom of the tenth with two outs and nobody on base. Fans were beginning to leave the stadium. A few Mets players had left the dugout and went into their locker room. NBC set up their cameras in the Boston Clubhouse. The Scoreboard prematurely congratulated The Red Sox as the world champions. It was then that Mets catcher Gary Carter hit a sharp single to left field for what would become a Hollywood comeback.

## ⊅ORTAL ⊂TO ⅄EAVEN

Remaining on the couch to watch a sure loss turn into an unforgettable, history-making victory cemented reinforced the quote by Yogi Berra who was both a Met and a Yankee: "It ain't over till it's over."

*Rejoice not against me, O mine enemy: when I fall, I shall arise…*

**Micah 7:8 (KJV)**

It was 2007. It was almost exactly 365 days before the 2008 Stock Market crash. For some reason, my small health care practice was determined to foreshadow that disaster a year early. I had used up a $200,000 line of credit when I went crawling back to the bank for more. They denied my request. I was up against a wall.

Could I sell my house to keep the practice afloat and prevent more layoffs? What was the answer?

Like films that coaches view, I relived my decisions over and over. I went into the books. I stared out windows. I began looking at staff performance. I stared out the window. I looked at the stock in our offices. And there it was: we were overstocked. Additionally, several staff jumped my sinking ship and our payroll dramatically dropped. Rather than rehire, I began to service the patients myself.

Within six months, we had paid off most of the line and were showing a half million dollars in the black. It was the wildest, quickest financial comeback I had ever experienced.

## PORTAL TO HEAVEN

God can prune several branches at once. I was the biggest one snipped. I had over-delegated, taken my eyes off the practice and moved away from seeing patients myself. On top of that, I had subtly bought into the idea that God would take care of things. I came back to my senses and Him. The comeback was in the "come back."

*...come back! Return to your God! You're down but you're not out. Prepare your confession and come back to God.*

**Hosea 14:1 (The Message)**

"Down, but not out."

We have all experienced some devastating blow and lived to see the morning. It's at these times that we begin looking for things to turn around. Sooner is better. But the "sooner" is never soon enough.

What happens when those mornings turn into weeks and the weeks turn into months and the months turn into years? Rolling out of bed becomes a routine of hope. Scripture says that "hope deferred makes the heart sick." This becomes more than a matter of patience. There are pivotal points during these desert years when the waiting on God stretches our faith to the point where there is a temptation to feel that we've been abandoned. In our heads, we know a perfect God would never do that. Yet, we feel alone.

Deserts also happen to countries. At one time, Israel's apostasy had led to its devastation and exile. Mothers eating their own babies during a siege…minor things like that. It's at this time that the prophet Jeremiah wrote some tough things to his people. They didn't listen.

## PORTAL TO HEAVEN

A paradox of the pen… With no hope left, Jeremiah scratches out on a scroll one of the most hopeful verses in all of scripture. It's the comeback before the comeback inspired by a God who already knows the end.

*The thought of my suffering and homelessness is bitter beyond words. I will never forget this awful time, as I grieve over my loss. Yet I still dare to hope when I remember this: The faithful love of the Lord never ends! His mercies never cease. Great is his faithfulness; his mercies begin afresh each morning. I say to myself, 'The Lord is my inheritance; therefore, I will hope in him!'*

**Jeremiah, in Lamentations 3:19-24 (NLT)**

# october
## PORTALS
## To HEAVEN

Autumn is a controversial season. Some love it. Some hate it. In the climate where I live, it brings in the harvest with apple pies and so much more. But the fall also portends bone-chilling days and nights, long spells of cabin fever and dangerous driving conditions. My hope comes through my appetite and taste buds.

There is a small apple orchard on our property. The apples are the crispiest and tastiest when you pick them right off the branch. They also infuse.

Why does God make us wait until autumn to bite into these apples and harvest many of our vegetables? Why does it coincide with colder temperatures and shorter days and with what for some is the most depressing time of the year because they must say goodbye to milder weather? He has His reasons.

We are the apple of His eye and we should consider a simple analogy.

The "autumn years" are the early senior years. For some, their fall comes far too soon. For others, their leaves are falling (translation: hair is thinning), their bark is worst than their bite, their limbs are not as strong as they used to be and the days are getting shorter as they take another step toward meeting their Maker.

## PORTAL TO HEAVEN

It is at this point in life that God expects a harvest of maturity. And, as in an orchard, He also anticipates a great variety of fruit.

*Even in old age they will still produce fruit; they will remain vital and green…*
*Keep me as the apple of Your eye…*

**Psalm 92:14 (NLT), Psalm 17:8 (NIV)**

Autumn can feel betraying if you enjoy warm weather. It can be sunny and 70 degrees and drop to 30 or 40 overnight.

Whether it's an apple or the cooler air, most describe it as crisp. Getting out for some fresh air in the fall is iconic. It could be moseying through your favorite orchard or corn maze or taking a hike to catch some breathtaking foliage if you live in the right climate and geography.

But there's something else in the autumn air. It's people.

Throughout their lives, my family and friends have provided me with a fresh air that's as real as a crisp October afternoon. What is it about a quick cup of java at a local coffee house, a phone conversation that leads to a refreshing outlook or some news they bring that we describe as a breath of fresh air?

Autumn's cooler temperature is awakening. You breathe deeply. It actually makes you feel healthier (barring allergies for some). It seems to spur the senses. It can clear the air of your emotions. It's the same with friends and family who stimulate you and make you feel part of the earth and the grander scheme of things.

And what of the colors of fall? They are like the kaleidoscope of looks, personalities and views of those we know intimately and those from we can only appreciate from a distance.

## ℗ORTAL ᲪTO ℌEAVEN

The colors, crispness and deliciousness of autumn are like the people who play a part in rescuing the fall from the first-frosts of life.

*There is a friend who sticks closer than a brother… Walk with the wise and become wise… a friend loves at all times and a brother is born for a time of adversity.*

**Proverbs 18:24b, 13:20, 17:17(ESV), (NLT), (NIV)**

The autumn sky is sometimes synonymous with the harvest moon where the lunar light shines so bright on successive nights that it gives stargazers the sense that they are seeing a few full moons in a row. It also rises a bit earlier so farmers get a few extra harvest hours.

The blood-red moon gives everyone a lot of reason to get excited because it turns red and looks like a gigantic beach ball that sits just beyond our backyards when it first rises.

The fall sky is so hard to miss. The morning star is ablaze with light and people are buzzing about how the stars can eclipse eclipses. What a show the stars put on in the autumn.

People look up to the stars because they are so supernatural. The sky bedazzles because it can throw a shooting star as you sit on your porch, display a glittering array during a romantic patio dance or seemingly schedule an extra full moon. The show never ends.

## PORTAL TO HEAVEN

The sky even gets into the act in the scriptures. The Bible tells us that we should resemble these heavenly bodies that put stars into the eyes of those we influence.

*Those who are wise will shine as bright as the sky, and those who lead many to righteousness will shine like the stars forever.*

**Daniel 12:3 (NLT)**

People from around the world come to visit northeastern America during the fall. While some locals may call our leaves pretty, out-of-towners term them stunning and worth every penny that they are charged at their B&B of choice.

Just after dawn, when the low-lying sun hits the foliage directly, the leaf peepers have it right. Our tulip tree's brilliant yellows in the early morning hours almost make me reach for my sunglasses while the maple across the yard throws just the right amount of reds into the mix so that visitors and upstaters exclaim October's coveted expression, "It's peak!"

Yet in just a few weeks, when the tourists are long gone and we are looking with contempt at those same leaves littering our lawns, we understand why it's called the fall.

## PORTAL TO HEAVEN

There are times when I will be able to glorify God in a way that may well be different in a few days, years or decades from now. But even at that, I hope that every day in every year will offer some measure of beauty that will give people reason to use the expression, "Stunning!"

*Blessed is the one who does not walk in step with the wicked or stand in the way that sinners take or sit in the company of mockers, but whose delight is in the law of the Lord, and who meditates on his law day and night. <u>That person is like a tree planted by streams of water, which yields its fruit in season and whose leaf does not wither</u>—whatever they do prospers.*

**Psalm 1:1-4 (NIV). Editor's emphasis.**

All good things must come to an end.

There's an ounce of both truth and fatalism in that expression. Usually, life doesn't just percolate endlessly like the old-fashioned pot of coffee that never tires of exuding its wonderful aroma.

And so it is with autumn. Heavy winds and driving rain can sweep away brilliant foliage almost overnight. You wake up and you'd think the naked trees should reach for a bathrobe. Besides going from wonderful colors to gray, we are faced with the fact that the deadness is going to be staring at us for a long time.

## PORTAL TO HEAVEN

Accept dead and/or dry times that we face as people of faith.
While not every barren time is caused by sin, deserts can certainly
be used for pruning and sometimes, like the winter, they seem
to go on forever.

Unlike the frosty season, we can't head to warmer climates for a few
months. We must face it. We must drink the delicious bitterness to
the bottom of the glass. It's only in this finishing work of God that
we move through repentance or pruning or both to the good
things of spring.

*Every branch in Me that does not bear fruit, He takes away; and every branch*
*that bears fruit, He prunes it so that it may bear more fruit.*

**John 15:2 (NAS)**

# PEN YOUR PORTALS

*(October is Pastor Appreciation Month.)*

I recognized the booming voice of my pastor during a Sunday school class from all the way down the hall. My ears were diverted from the lesson for a split second and then safely returned to my teacher. In that moment, however, I grasped in full measure the metaphor of the voice of a shepherd.

One of the most endearing self-described titles of Christ is that of a shepherd.

Hearing Pastor's voice harkened to the time when I heard that same voice repent of not following Christ's discipleship-model for the church. It was as if Pastor was saying, "The shepherd must change before the sheep can."

His call from the pulpit at that time was a return to the New Testament model of discipleship: small-group meetings in homes, accountability and all the specific directives of the original Shepherd and his under-shepherds that we now call the first Apostles.

But the voice of a shepherd doesn't just bark out directions. He must walk ahead and find pasture. Pastor did that by making radical changes in his lifestyle that enabled him to follow his shepherd into the greener pastures of discipling several men who are now elders and under-shepherds.

## PORTAL TO HEAVEN

A true shepherd's path will be well-worn. His voice represents the call of The Shepherd.

*My sheep hear my voice, and I know them, and they follow me ... I have other sheep that are not of this sheep pen. I must bring them also. They too will listen to my voice, and there shall be one flock and one shepherd.*

**John 10:27 (ESV), John 10:16 (NLT)**

*(October is Pastor Appreciation Month.)*

"Go for it!" Pastor said. "I think it's a great idea."

This is the voice of a confident and secure pastor who is not afraid to release men and women into their calling while building community through works within and outside the church.

In my case as a music minister, Pastor released me to grow a worship community. As a result, the church expanded to three worship teams.

Others have followed Pastor's voice of release and it has led to church members being outwardly focused as well as inwardly secure.

One congregant had a tremendous background in apologetics and engineering. In part because of Pastor's encouragement, this man teamed up with the local YMCA and a couple of hundred attendees sat on their ice rink listening to many convincing proofs of the resurrection.

One elder whom Pastor discipled had grown up in the Jewish faith. As he matured in his walk, he increasingly began to recognize all of the symbols and nuances of the Passover meal. He now teaches these insights at an annual Seder, which draws hundreds of participants.

## ꓑORTAL ꓖTO ꓯEAVEN

Pastor heard his Shepherd say, "Go for it" and now he is saying the same to his flock.

---

*Truly, truly, I tell you, whoever believes in Me will also do the works that I am doing. He will do even greater things than these, because I am going to the Father.*

**John 14:12 (BSB)**

*(October is Pastor Appreciation Month.)*

I was just getting ready to leave after Pastor's Sunday morning benediction. As he walked off the stage, I was struck with the sense that his sermon could have leveled Goliath and a few demons at the same time. Goliath would have definitely heard Pastor's voice from across the valley.

But it's not his commanding voice alone that warrants respect. It's the authority with which he delivers sermons, bible studies and the like. The synoptic gospels of Matthew, Mark and Luke harmonize with perfect pitch. Why was authority so critical and relevant to these three scribes of the gospels? It's obvious that they had been subjected to more lame shepherds' voices - just as in our day.

Pastor's boom isn't measured merely in decibels. His careful and diligent studying of The Bible and his subsequent teachings remove any doubt as to which Shepherd he is following. It is this bedrock that has helped create the ethos of our spiritual community.

## PORTAL TO HEAVEN

It's easier for us to recognize the metaphor of the shepherd's voice the way Christ's early followers did when the instructions from a pulpit boom with the authority that comes from reading and studying the letters in red.

Matthew, Mark and Luke made sure they signed up in triplicate:
*He taught with real authority – quite unlike their teachers of religious law…The people were amazed at his teaching, for he taught with real authority – quite unlike the teachers of religious law…There, too, the people were amazed at his teaching, for he spoke with authority.*

**Luke 4:32 (NLT), Matthew 7:29 (NLT), Mark 1:22 (NLT)**

*(October is Pastor Appreciation Month.)*

Pastors are referred to as shepherds in the Bible. These days, we don't see many of sheep-herders in the suburbs. However, I did have the chance to study some shepherds while visiting Israel. Their sheep listen to their voices.

The dual role of a shepherd is to employ both sides of the shepherd's staff to keep the flock moving toward safe and plentiful pastures.

Liken this to the voice of encouragement from my pastor that comes in many forms. There is the obvious: "Great job!" "Stay the course!" "You're a blessing!"

Though harder to take, shepherds also have to deliver harder words. Properly and sensitively said, these admonitions are the very medicine that attack a propensity, sin or a simple error in thought or direction.

Pastor also employs a great deal of encouragement by simply being unrelenting in his focus of Jesus – particularly by preaching that Christ was crucified for all of the things that Satan is constantly trying to remind us of.

In Israel, I saw a shepherd wait 20 minutes for a sheep that wandered into some thickets. He had time for that one lamb. Pastor, despite his busy schedule, is always willing to meet.

## ᑭORTAL ᏩTO ᕼEAVEN

There really is a shepherd in the suburbs. If you don't have one, search for him. Hopefully, he'd be the type that would search for you if you got lost in some thickets.

*Then I will give you shepherds after my own heart, who will lead you with knowledge and understanding.*

**Jeremiah 3:15 (NLT)**

*(October is Pastor Appreciation Month.)*

In biblical times, there was loaded imagery through the metaphor of the shepherd and sheep.

Today, we might use other symbolism that would compare pastors with a traffic cop directing cars, a trainer at a gym motivating clients, a teacher moving a class through world history or a C.E.O. governing each division of a company. Back in the day, however, the shepherding analogy was a clear picture of leadership, guidance and self-sacrifice.

My pastor is one of those guys.

I have witnessed his downsizing, sharing of the pulpit, willingness to shed duties in order to disciple and mentor, his travel on mission trips to preach in oppressive heat and walking-his-talk way out of his comfort zone in many areas.

Shepherds start paths. If he were to look behind him, he would see some assisting-shepherds managing a group of us because they trust his leadership.

## PORTAL TO HEAVEN

Seeing the similarity of this obedient shepherd with that of The Good Shepherd who steadfastly and unswervingly walked His talk straight down His Father's path to the cross. Imagery may change with time. But whatever metaphor you come up with, it would have to be of someone who is willing to lay down his life for others.

*And it came to pass, when the time was come that [Jesus] should be received up, he steadfastly set his face to go to Jerusalem...When [The Good Shepherd] has brought out all his own, he goes on ahead of them*

**Luke 9:51(KJB), John 10:4 (NIV). Editor's Brackets.**

"Fear 101" seems to be a prerequisite course in the University of Life.

As a student who had to repeat these studies a few times and who tends to think that going back and auditing the class somehow garners me some extra credit, I can reveal the fear that seems to sit at the top of this syllabus: "The Fear of Being Alone."

Some say they prefer to be alone. What they are really saying is that they like to be alone sometimes. I don't know of anyone who wishes they had never met anyone and who wants to be alone now and for eternity. Even if some unique person expressed that, it would carry dishonesty with it because they wouldn't know the full effect that eternity could play on their aloneness.

I must make a sharp turn from the abstract and return to the campus where we begin to dissect the syllabus.

One of the first lessons in "The Fear of Being Alone" is the utter nightmare of being separated from God. Even the most ardent atheist will admit that if they live long enough, they will outlive *all* of their friends. They would truly be alone because they have no God.

On the other hand, the God-believer would be terrified at the thought of separation from God because they already know what it is to be connected with the one in whose image they were made.

## PORTAL TO HEAVEN
To lose God *is* hell.

*And be sure of this: I am with you always, even to the end of the age.*

**Matthew 28:20 (NLT)**

The prospect of being permanently alone either now or eternally tops my list of fears. Even the strictest monks have fellowship with one another and God.

This has led me to the conclusion that it is not good for man to be alone. I think I've read that somewhere before.

In my life, there did come a time when the only hug I could give was to my pillow. Staring at the ceiling one night before finally drifting off, I had a vision of a man meeting with a king. He was surprised that the king was so jovial.

He was even more jolted by the king's personal interest and knowledge of him; and not just of the present, but of his entire life. I wrote it down in what would become the short story at the beginning of the journal, *The King's Favorite Book.* *

We won't ruin the ending. It is something everyone should read. The King's Favorite Book is every person's story.

*"The King's Favorite Book" © 2006, Robert J. LaCosta. See Products Page at the back of this book.*

## ᏢORTAL ᏟTO ᎻEAVEN

Even when the pillow seems to be your only friend, rest on the cushion of the reality of God's presence – whether in the dullness of your unfortunate wakefulness or in the alertness of your dreams.

*For I am sure that neither death nor life, nor angels nor rulers, nor things present nor things to come, nor powers, nor height nor depth, nor anything else in all creation, will be able to separate us from the love of God in Christ Jesus our Lord... Even though I walk through the valley of the shadow of death, I will fear no evil, for you are with me.*

**Romans 8:38,39 (ESV), Psalm 23:4 (ESV)**

I've always been a bit sensitive to the early warning systems of my body. If the slightest thing bothered me, I'd wonder what's going on. To be honest, there have been times when I feared the worst. Some fears could be drawn from a family history whereby I'd worry if whatever befell grandparents or Mom or Dad would visit me.

As I got older, I never hesitated to go to the doctor. At some points, I mused as to whether he felt that I was a hypochondriac. He never showed any signs of disrespect. In fact, just to be safe, he would often send me off to a specialist. I have a very thick three-ring binder tracking my medical visits and outcomes. I try to stay abreast without obsessing. As a hearing health practitioner, this scenario plays out in reverse. I had the opportunity to reassure an elderly woman that fear of death is a normal concern and that most people would be lying if they never had an anxious thought regarding the subject. I had to listen to my own advice.

However long I live, I pull great confidence from the hundreds of times that Christ has healed me over my life and the myriad of recorded times when He stopped to take care of the sick and diseased and the worrywarts. So, when I fear the worst, I use the very compassion of Jesus to defeat my fear.

## ᑭORTAL ᏟTO ᕼEAVEN

Leaning into the very character of Christ abates my fear because of his track record of taking care of me. This would be analogous to the kid who gets ice cream for that wretched soar throat…
or something like that.

*So do not fear, for I am with you; do not be dismayed, for I am your God. I will strengthen you and help you… Jesus said to Jairus, 'Don't be afraid'… Lord my God, I called to you for help, and you healed me… Then they cried to the Lord in their trouble…He sent out his word and healed them.*

**Isaiah 41:10, Luke 8:50a, Psalm 30:2, Psalm 107:19ff (NIV)**

Picture Jesus with an Italian-Brooklyn accent telling you,"Don't worry abboudit!" Growing up in the New York City area, I would hear this expression and wonder how people like that could be so confident.

Financially fearful as I grew up, I was always waiting for the other shoe to drop.

It stemmed from the typical concerns of a big family with a small budget. Actually, Mom and Dad did a great job of providing – even down to scrounging up an extra nickel for orange drink (instead of plain milk) in those little cartons at the elementary school. However,"We can't afford that" got embedded into my sensitive and understanding psyche. I virtually accepted it as the rule of thumb. Anything more would be a pleasant surprise.

Waiting for the shoe to drop walked me through many of my adult years. Upon college graduation, I watched many friends get better paying jobs than me. I had grown to expect a lower, modest salary. But life is like a pendulum and my financial situation radically changed for the good. Yet, I still had this nagging sense.

## PORTAL TO HEAVEN

God's provision remains during the lows and highs. If Jesus was giving the Sermon on the Mount in Brooklyn, he would probably use the colloquial,"Don't worry abboudit." If I were in the audience, he'd tell me to stop worrying about the shoe dropping and start putting my foot down when it came to "worrying abboudit."

*I tella you notta to worry abat you life. Don'ta a worry abathavin' sometin to eat or drinka or weara...*

**Matthew 6:25 (The Italian-Jesus-From-Brooklyn Version)**

"The only thing we have to fear is fear itself," said President Franklin D. Roosevelt in his first inaugural address that spoke to the heart of those suffering from the effects of The Great Depression.

Though he brought confidence to his nation, Roosevelt had been literally paralyzed with fear due to his polio which left him without use of much of his legs. Overcoming through arduous physical rehabilitation, his wife said he never again succumbed to being fearful after conquering the anxiety of polio.

## ᏢORTAL ᏟᎢO ᎨEAVEN

Roosevelt overcame worry by the very thing he feared the most. It behooves us to look at our worst anxieties and rehabilitate them through the counsel of God and those He assigns as therapists: spouses, family, friends, counselors, faith-community leaders and the like. If you would like to take the first step, print out in duplicate the following contract. Sign and date both and keep one for your file or frame it and post on a wall. Mail the other as an act of faith to someone you trust who will most likely outlive you. Remember Roosevelt…and go ahead, sign *The No-Fear Contract:*

*Even though I walk through the valley of the shadow of death,*
*I will fear no evil, for you are with me; your rod and your staff, they comfort*
*me… I prayed to the Lord, and he answered me. He freed me from all my*
*fears… And I am convinced that nothing can ever separate us from God's*
*love. Neither death nor life, neither angels nor demons, neither our fears for*
*today nor our worries about tomorrow—not even the powers of hell can*
*separate us from God's love.*

**Psalm 23:4 (ESV), Psalm 34:4 (NLT), Romans 8:38,39 (NLT)**

# ◯NO-FEAR-CONTRACT

I've walked the path of worry so many times before

And every time fret beckoned, I opened wide my door.

Whether I was outside or fortified at home,

Anxiety had permission to roar and freely roam.

How much time I've wasted and energy given away

To this undeserving beast who never earns his pray.

And now You've offered me a life that's free from fear,

A contract without small print, I'll sign that gladly, here:

_____          _____
(NAME)                                      (DATE)

# PEN YOUR PORTALS

"Now children, what is the pattern in the pictures below?" asks the elementary teacher. If grade school kids can get patterns, there's a shot I can catch on as well.

I have been intrigued by portals to heaven – those things that are the subtle or overt symbols or metaphors of heaven that daily point to heaven. Patterns or types can be portals.

Probably because of my gender, one of the most exciting types of patterns in this world is the role of a father. In Judeo-Christian belief, the concept of fatherhood is a revered window into the reality of God the Father. No pressure, dads.

Despite some of our failings as dads, we do get the picture. Providing, caring, correcting, disciplining, guiding, restoring, giving in (just seeing if you were paying attention) and hugging are some of the aspects of our job description.

I loved being a young father. I love being an older father. Regarding the latter, my experience in the field of aging has shown me that the 90-year-old dad or mom never stops being a parent. It's built-in no matter how old (or fresh) your kids get. It is hard, however, to spank a 65-year-old son or daughter.

## PORTAL TO HEAVEN

On the other side of this life, we'll see that this patterned privilege not only followed us to the grave, it led us there.

*I kneel before the Father, from whom every family in heaven and on earth derives its name…I pray that you… grasp how wide and long and high and deep is the love of Christ, and to know this love that surpasses knowledge – that you may be filled to the measure of all the fullness of God [the Father].*

**Ephesians 3:14, 18,19 (NIV), Editor's bracket.**

Perhaps the greatest pattern that points people to the specific character and aspects of God is found in the family. These are the hands we were meant to hold onto for dear life. One was my now deceased dad.

I was seven at the New York World's Fair. Though I didn't understand that there were tens of thousands in attendance, I distinctly remember being swept through the gates at the entrance as Mom excitedly talked about the Ford and the General Motors exhibits that purportedly had some of the most modern displays. At the fair's epicenter stood a huge metallic globe. Through my young eyes, it was as big as the earth.

It was within this humongous backdrop of grandness and distraction that I found myself holding the hand of a man about half the size of that globe. I burst into tears. For a brief second, I was drowning in a sea of thousands of strangers. Within seconds, I saw Dad smiling and waving apologetically at the man while trying to reassure me that I didn't fall off the globe of security.

## ᏢORTAL ᏳTO ᎻEAVEN

I was never really out of Dad's sight – but, oh, did it ever feel like it.

*Yet for us there is but one God, the Father, from whom are all things and we exist for Him; and one Lord, Jesus Christ, by whom are all things, and we exist through Him.*

**1 Corinthians 8:6 (NIV)**

Dad passed away years ago.

While photographs and even some old videos can serve to retain images of the real-life guy who used to hug me and scrape me with his whiskers, pictures just aren't the same.

But just last night, I was visited by Dad's double or was it…?

I was sitting at my office desk with others milling around. As I turned, I noticed an older man behind me looking at me with a big and steady smile. It was a double of my dad. I was floored. I announced to everyone, "This man is an exact double of my dad!" I went over to him. I looked him in the eyes and said, "I don't know who you are, but I love you!" I hugged him so deeply and said, "You have brown eyes and my dad had blue, but that will have to do." He smiled and began to say something about me.

I woke up. Wait! What was he going to say? I wanted so badly to return to the dream. Looking out the window from my bed, I could see the beautiful backlit-by-clouds crescent moon lazily hanging above his appointed stars.

I asked God about the dream. It seems that our parents are supposed to be good patterns – like the kind in sewing. Dad was a good worker. Standing behind me with that big smile, it was as if he was saying, "I'm right behind you in your work."

## PORTAL TO HEAVEN

It is a pattern of God to provide an experience that beats even the best photos on the wall. I get the picture.

*May the LORD watch between you and me when we are absent one from the other…Follow God's example, therefore, as dearly loved children…*

**Genesis 31:49 (NIV), Ephesians 5:1 (NIV)**

Our New Jersey family of nine visited the Statue of Liberty on a hot summer day with all of the pride that comes with the children and grandchildren of immigrants. Many of the ethnic groups that now have been thoroughly mixed in the melting pot were much closer to her bosom back then. Moreover, she raised her torch in our backyard; she was hard to mis...understand.

I was a small child and 354 stairs were a lot to ask of me. I might have made 10 before my white flag was raised – as were my arms toward my dad in a pleading motion.

He obliged by putting me on his shoulders. My stubby little hands could feel the heat radiating from his red-hot forehead before we were even half way up.

I had the sense that my dad was some kind of super hero, a type which the colossal statue represented. When we made it the observatory crown, I was sure he was Superman.

## PORTAL TO HEAVEN

Fathers, especially those who are sons of immigrants, give us a pattern of the uphill climb of hard labor and of making the foreign known. While I had a literal ride, "imports" like us figuratively stand on the shoulders of those brave souls. I have no memory of the magnificent view from Lady Liberty's crown. I can only remember being carried on his shoulders. That view remains.

*You saw how the Lord your God carried you, just as a man carries his son, in all the way which you have walked until you came to this place...When he has found [the sheep], he lays it on his shoulders, rejoicing.*

**Deuteronomy 1:31 (NIV), Luke 15:5 (NASB) [Editor's brackets]**

Cash flow was never a friend of my parents. We weren't broke even though it quite often sounded like that. Looking back, it was probably the normal wear and tear on the checking account of a family of nine.

I was toward the bottom of the line sequentially and I remember my dad more as an older man. He married at forty and I didn't come around until he was fifty and I really didn't have any concept about finances until he was nearing retirement age. It was at that point that I heard him repeatedly say, "If I could just figure out how to make some money."

In retrospect, it was his concern for Mom and the seven kids that brought this worry out into the open. Having worked with seniors all of my life, I can tell you that the anxiety of outliving your savings is a burden – especially if college is still on the horizon for some of your kids.

## PORTAL TO HEAVEN

The pattern of dad's provision is that same reassurance that Jesus taught when he spoke of the "birds of the air" being fed. Some of dad's work-ethic sweat fell on each of us and for the right reason: to provide.

Like billions before him, Dad died concerning himself about money and that was unfortunate. However, he intrinsically patterned himself after his Heavenly Father more than he knew. When he passed, my share of his estate went to a down payment on a house that granddaughters who never knew him enjoyed all their growing years.

*A good man leaveth an inheritance to his children's children... Look at the birds of the air, that they do not sow, nor reap nor gather into barns, and yet your heavenly Father feeds them. Are you not worth much more than they?*

**Proverbs 13:22 (KJV), Mt. 6:26 (NIV)**

I love graveyards.

There are no airs there-even in Harvard Square's cemetery.

There are no heirs there either, for it is said that God has no grandchildren.

There is only death and that is why I like to call them graveyards rather than cemeteries. While that may be of a more grave term, it is more honest and accurate.

The word cemetery comes from the idea of bedding down, lying down, sleeping, as in a dormitory.

In all my years of walking or biking through cemeteries, I've never once seen anyone get up from their nap.

No, it's "graveyard" for me because we are all sentenced to death. The body's death is the final one on this earth, but that's just a bookend to God's grave plot regarding worldly things.

## ᑭORTAL ᑕTO ᕼEAVEN

God writes up a long list of life's deaths. One after another, day after day, every step we take brings on another death and gets us one step closer to my physical death.

"We were born to die," the saying goes.

There's no place for morbidity here. Rather, there's life for the taking.

*For we died and were buried with Christ by baptism. And just as Christ was raised from the dead by the glorious power of the Father, now we also may live new lives.*

**Romans 6:4 (NLT)**

Call me an escapist, but I'm down with spending some time with these silent types.

You don't have to be walking through a cemetery to realize that there is a peace that comes with death – especially the kind of mortification that follows when I die to my whims and wishes.

It is said that the best soldiers are those who have already died because they are dead men walking and the fear of death is behind them. I'm not sure how many completely live this out, but the analogy is sure there for those looking to battle for God rather than preserve their own lives. Those enlisted in military service don't have the choice to talk back to their commanding officer. This is the peace that these graveyard warriors have discovered.

## PORTAL TO HEAVEN

The lack of discussion with these "silent types" proves that there is a peace that comes from having nothing to say about your current condition – even when you're feeling a little under it.

*I plead with you to give your bodies to God because of all he has done for you. Let them be a living and holy sacrifice – the kind he will find acceptable. This is truly the way to worship him…Do not repay evil with evil or insult with insult…repay evil with blessing…seek peace and pursue it…A person's wisdom yields patience; it is to one's glory to overlook an offense.*

**Romans 12:1 (NLT), 1 Peter 3:9-11 (excerpted), Proverbs 19:11 (NIV)**

When I return to my home state, I'll sometimes stop by to visit with my parents. They've been gone for decades, so the graveyard is as close as I can get... or is it?

My memory of them has grown so thin that I start to wonder, "How much am I like them in the way I act, feel and how I handle life at this current stage?"

My graveyard chat receives no replies except when I notice the dash. It makes me think of "The Dash," a poem by Linda Ellis that speaks about the time between the dates on gravestones as the symbol of who we will always be – not just the who-we-were or what-we-accomplished.

That's the answer I get from these visits. That's the answer I need.

While specific recollections are dissolving, I recall their giving nature, character and countenance and I am aware that they have passed that down to us kids.

## PORTAL TO HEAVEN

The "gave-stone" over the plot is indeed a marker in my life. It's a memorial as solid as the granite that bears their name it will forever remind me of who I am and from whence I came. And it speaks of another rock...

*I bow my knees before the Father, from whom every family in heaven and on earth derives its name ...we have all had human fathers who disciplined us and we respected them for it. How much more should we submit to the Father of spirits and live!... the rock was Christ.*

**Ephesians 3:14 (NIV), Hebrews 12:9 (NIV),
1 Corinthians 10:4 (ESV)**

Question: Why are there always fences around cemeteries?

Answer: People are dying to get in.

That first-grade joke may be applied to many of the things that anyone can get caught up in on a daily basis. The things that lead to death are always out there. They are like the graveyards that we pass every day.

The analogy is that the temptations of the world are still the things that take men and women down on any given day. If we could see how people have died spiritually and what did them in, we'd see what Scripture calls "the world, the flesh and the devil."

Some examples from these three are things of the world's system such as notoriety or prestige and respect and being driven by money or "stuff." These are the things the world says are important.

The "flesh" includes those instincts that gratify our bodies or minds in such a way that are diametrically opposed to God's laws. The devil always wants to lure us into the graveyard of dreams, desires, perversions and a whole gamut of sins that will put us in the spiritual grave.

## PORTAL TO HEAVEN

Jesus promised to leave us The Holy Spirit who is the counselor. He will reveal those things in our lives that lead to life and those that lead to tragic burials. Thank God for analogous first-grade jokes.

*For the gate is wide and the way is easy that leads to destruction, and those who enter by it are many.*

**Matthew 7:13 (ESV)**

Walking through a graveyard is like going through a dress rehearsal. I feel like I'm preparing to die. Before you think "Morbid!" hear me out.

Many will agree that the secret to life is to walk in the footsteps of Jesus. His ordered and determined steps would often bring up questions, rebukes, confusion and sorrow from those trying to follow in His steps because of incessant talks about His death. That is where He was headed His entire life: to die that we might live. Yes, He was born to die. Jesus is talking about His death and nobody says He's morbid.

Peter told Jesus not to "walk and talk" about death. Jesus rebuked Peter – and Satan – in one breath. Thomas awkwardly asked, "We have no idea where you are going, so how can we know the way?" Peter also declared, "Even if I have to die with you, I will never disown you. And all the other disciples said the same."

## PORTAL TO HEAVEN

Each of my steps on earth is taking me to the same place that these souls below my feet have gone: death. But the death that Jesus spoke about is one of life. With every step, I'm practicing as in a dress rehearsal the death of Christ by following Him. By doing this, irony of ironies, I'm walking straight toward my empty grave.

*Christ suffered for our sins once for all time. He never sinned, but he died for sinners to bring you safely home to God. He suffered physical death, but he was raised to life in the Spirit.*

**1 Peter 3:18 (NLT)**

# November
## PORTALS
## To Heaven

He was tall for his age. It seemed to give him better vision. It was as if he could see further than his compatriots. Yet he told me that he was practically starving where he was.

It seemed that he was always looking for the next break, something that would finally put some food on the table.

There were trees with green leaves everywhere he looked. Beautiful, delicious. What a view!

He would tell all of his friends. But they couldn't see what he saw and they labeled him a dreamer. Every time he'd stick his neck out, opportunity was just out of his reach. His friends were getting fat right where they were. Oh, what was his problem?

Meanwhile, his best friend was wondering about his behavior. There was plenty right in front of him. The only thing his friend could figure was that he was a visionary with myopia. He could see all of the potential of his ideas, but couldn't see his own provision.

Finally, his friend removed the roof over the shed so that the tall guy's provision was clearly in sight. He had been too busy reaching for the branches of the trees outside his pen to see the provision his best friend had been laying out every afternoon.

It was at this point that he saw all of the branches and leaves that his best friend had been providing every day.

## PORTAL TO HEAVEN

The giraffe stopped craning his neck over the fence and humbly moved toward the delicious meal that had been waiting for him all along.

*Your Father knows what you need before you ask him.*

**Matthew 6:8 (NIV)**

While I'm not exactly mechanically-inclined or tech-savvy, I have had some minor accomplishments in my duties as a homeowner.

For example, some mice decided to turn my stove into an apartment complex. I got right on it at 10 p.m., but all of the stores were closed by then and I had to scrounge around for whatever was needed.

I took the grill off only to discover I couldn't do anything without a micro hexagon ratchet. Lacking any real hope, I went down to the basement and searched through every tool I had. I miraculously found a hex set that I had never used in my life.

Provision often comes through a series of seemingly disconnected small steps of trust and faith. I had never taken apart a stove. My nose was telling me I'd better. My pocketbook was telling me I couldn't call a repairman. I backed my way into the job and was forced at every step of this smelly journey to simply trust God for the next insight, tool and wisdom to clean up the effects of the unwanted tenants.

## PORTAL TO HEAVEN

The provision didn't come through a credit card, a new stove or even a repairman. It only came as I took a step into the unknown world of an evicting landlord.

*I will instruct you and teach you in the way you should go;*
*I will counsel you with my eye upon you.*

**Psalm 32:8 (NIV)**

**Also read: Proverbs 3:5 (NIV)**

I was walking past some of the gardens in my house and I realized that the hostas, ferns and tulips were in their full glory and I had never thrown one seed. Perennials pop up all over. They tend to be the most amazing because they are like an employee who shows up for work and never asks for a paycheck.

Like the world of investment, compound interest is where money grows over a long period of time.

I still get a kick when I haven't been around for a week or so and the garden mysteriously fills in all by itself.

The previous owners lived here for seven decades. In that time, they made some good choices and the evidence of their forethought is obvious and beautiful.

But could you imagine planting only vines and poison ivy and walking by and seeing a lush garden spring up?

## PORTAL TO HEAVEN

God made an investment in the Garden. While Adam misspent Papa's fortune, The Second Adam came along and made an investment that's still paying the most astounding interest ever recorded.

*For the wages of sin is death…[But] you were bought with a price …*
*So glorify God … They receive God's approval freely by an act of his kindness*
*through the price Christ Jesus paid to set us free [from sin]… For even the*
*Son of Man did not come to be served, but to serve, and to give his*
*life as a ransom for many.*

**Romans 6:23 (ESV), 1 Corinthians 6:20 (ESV), Romans 3:23 (GWT), Mark 10:45 (NIV)**

There was a point during the renovation of our historic Hudson River home when one wrong move could tragically damage the beautiful old wallpaper that I was desperately hoping to save.

The contractors were well aware of my wallpaper wishes. Their care was nothing short of heroic. But when it came to adding a staircase to access an almost unreachable attic, some of the walls with wallpaper had to go.

My heroes hired a painter who matched the wallpaper with a stellar recreation of the vintage design! I had to point out to visitors the difference between her mural parts and the actual wallpaper. I was proud that we "pulled that off," but it was an expensive caper!

A couple of years later, I was rummaging around the basement and stumbled upon my version of the Dead Sea Scrolls. It was four perfect rolls of that exact same wallpaper. In that dark corner of the basement I discovered that mistakes could become provision.

## PORTAL TO HEAVEN

We sometimes miss an already-provided provision. Hopefully we won't make that error again. And that's the portal to heaven called redemption.

*'You are not yet fifty years old,' they said to him, 'and you have seen Abraham!'... For if these things are done when the tree is green, what will happen when it is dry?... None of the rulers of this age understood it, for if they had, they would not have crucified the Lord of glory.*

**John 8:57 (NIV), Luke 23:31 (NLT), 1 Corinthians 2:8 (NIV)**

**Also read: John 20:15 (The Message)**

"Time is all we have" is an old saying that bears repeating.

But once time is lost, who can replace it? Is there a way God can somehow give us a provision to make up for lost time?

I have noticed how He directly intervenes to give me some extra time. I use this term only to reflect His cleverness, not in some spooky way.

For example, I've been observing that if I'm standing around, I may not be in tune with how God wants me to use that moment. If there are not dirty dishes that need attention, there are usually clean ones in the dishwasher that are a hidden opportunity to gain some extra time while I'm waiting for my English muffin to pop up. Moreover, I crank my stereo and listen to The One Year Bible that seems to make time fly.

## PORTAL TO HEAVEN

God may be doing something in our lives that seems as innocuous as a cancelled appointment, someone running late, or even an emergency. We plan our day; He directs the steps.

Look for these little, sometimes seemingly insignificant shifts in schedules. Perhaps He's showing you that the saying, "Time is all we have," should be changed to "Time is what God gives."

*The preparations of the heart belong to man, but the answer of the tongue is from the Lord... A man's heart plans his way, but the Lord directs his steps.*

**Proverbs 16:1,9 (NKJV)**

It had been the most harrowing financial year for our rapidly growing business. A bloated staff, a rough economy, a slow-down in new patients and my inexperience as a C.E.O. led to a disastrous three quarters.

With the holidays looming, the situation had not changed. I began making cuts. I was literally sick to my stomach. I pray that you never, ever have to fire a single soul.

What had always been one of my favorite holidays was now shrouded in un-thankfulness. I had always loved Thanksgiving. Growing up in a big family, it was lasagna, turkey and lots of family and friends and even more Tums. I had kept that tradition throughout adulthood.

I made a habit of journaling thankful thoughts over the years. But this year, there was a cloud over my pen. Since I couldn't find anything to write about, I decided to review what I had written regarding gratefulness.

On the title page I had written, "The lines have fallen to me in pleasant places; indeed, my heritage is beautiful to me. Psalm 16:6."

Tears cascaded as I turned each page and read about the faithfulness of God in my life.

## PORTAL TO HEAVEN

Thanksgiving and giving thanks have everything to do with the care and love of God and little to do with circumstance.

*In everything give thanks; for this is God's will for you in Christ Jesus.*

**1 Thessalonians 5:18 (NAS)**

"The Puritan writer John Flavel points out in his book, *The Mystery of Providence,* 'Without due observation of the works of Providence no praise can be rendered to God for any of them. It is our duty to meditate upon these works at all times, but especially in times of difficulty and trouble.' By observation, Flavel means to specifically record the works, care and mercies God has shown us. We need to look at life carefully. Think about God's care. Write down the evidence. I am amazed by my own ability to forget so quickly. I can never count on my memory when I most need to consider the faithfulness of the Lord. I must record the work of God or it is gone forever." (Margie Haack, *WORLD Magazine.*)

Haack's admission matches my own. I forget so easily.

I could forget the great parking space outside the grocery store within a few minutes of getting stuck with the slowest cashier.

Deliberate efforts to see God's goodness in everyday life significantly improve our chances of seeing portals to heaven.

## PORTAL TO HEAVEN

Recognize that Flavel was right and a flippant attitude toward anything is wicked. Moreover, the decision not to be diligent in actively and constantly recording in our mind and on paper the bountiful blessings of God and His perfect character and motivation is worse.

*I will remember the works of the Lord; surely I will remember Your wonders of old. I will also meditate on all Your work, and talk of Your deeds.*

**Psalm 77:11,12. (NAS)**
**Also read: Colossians 4:2, Hebrews 13:15**

I wish I could produce a reality show of testimonies of thankfulness. We would never run out of footage.

The Bible is really one example after another of God's faithfulness. Even in the depressing, morbid and sinful biblical accounts, scripture is replete with man bumping up against the purity and perfection of God.

It's one thing to be thankful during the good times. But thanksgiving to God seems to be infinitely more valuable when it's offered during bad times. My mind wanders to the prayer of thanks of the great scholar Matthew Henry after he was robbed.

"I thank thee, first because I was never robbed before; second, because altho' they took my belongings, they did not take my life; third, altho' they took everything I had, it was not much; and fourth, because it was I who was robbed, not I who robbed."

Although a reality show may never record a robbery like that on camera, Henry was forever caught in the act of thanksgiving through his words.

I have not yet mastered this thanksgiving thing.

## ᑭORTAL ᒍO ᕼEAVEN

We must master thanksgiving because it is the very oxygen of heaven.

*And the twenty-four elders who sat before God on their thrones fell on their faces and worshiped God, saying: 'We give You thanks, O Lord God Almighty, the One who is and who was and who is to come, because You have taken Your great power and reigned.'*

**Revelation 11:16-17 (KJV)**

"Why, sometimes I've believed as many as six impossible things before breakfast." When I first read this quote by Lewis Carroll, his enthusiasm challenged me to declare in faith, "Why sometimes I've thanked God for 60 things before breakfast – and an early breakfast at that."

I decided to try it and it turned out to be easier than I thought. In fact, I was done in minutes after a flurry of stream-of-consciousness thank-you's. Whew!

The reason for the ease was that there is so much for which to thank God at any given moment. However, the gauntlet is not in that fact.

It's the circumstances and daily irritations that swirl around us like autumn leaves on a windy day.

And so, the utter determination of the old hymn "Count Your Blessings" by Oatman and Excell must win the day: "Count your many blessings; name them one by one, and it will surprise you what the Lord has done."

## ₽ORTAL ᏟᎢᎾ ₤EAVEN

Try "The 10,000 Challenge." Head toward 10,000 reasons to thank God. Begin by journaling your blessings each day or week. If these translated into money, you'd find that you're indeed very wealthy.

*From the rising of the sun to its setting The name of the Lord is to be praised... I will bless the Lord at all times; His praise shall continually be in my mouth.... My mouth is filled with Your praise And with Your glory all day long... give thanks in all circumstances.*

**Psalm 113:3 (ESV), Psalm 34:1 (ESV), Psalm 71:8 (ESV),
1 Thessalonians 5:18 (ESV)**

"Count your many blessings; name them one by one, and it will surprise you what the Lord has done." So the hymn goes.

But if we are counting silently, how will God get the credit?

For instance, I was so thankful about the sale of my business. I was just uncertain how to talk about this offer that no one could refuse. My hesitation was based in the fear of the appearance of bragging.

Later, I realized that I was to give God glory because that deal had nothing to do with me; it was God who brought that arrangement together with its subsequent financial and other blessings.

God was not getting any glory through my silence. By not testifying of the amazing God-incidences, such as the timing, finances and the opportunity to transition into a writing ministry, I was robbing people of learning about the wonders of His way.

Sharing is not the same thing as boasting if it's done in a manner that passes praise right through to God or another whose assistance made possible the mazel-tov moment.

## PORTAL TO HEAVEN

Verbal expressions are built into the habit of thanksgiving. Let's not be turkeys when it comes to relating our thanksgiving. You can brag on God anytime you want.

*That is why I can never stop praising you; I declare your glory all day long… Let them praise the LORD for his great love and for the wonderful things he has done for them.*

**Psalm 71:8 (NLT), Psalm 107:31 (NLT)**

For many years, I had wanted to write in either a professional sense or as an avocation. But I was financially strapped and didn't even have a computer. God also put another obstacle in my path: a career ... or so it seemed. I distinctly remember resenting my boss and the time my job took away from my passion for writing.

I decided to be accountable to God. I began logging my work hours versus writing hours. By looking at my dishonesty on paper, I began holding myself to a higher standard. It was a turn-around in my career and an ethical breakthrough. My diligence was noticed by my boss and he eventually sold me his hearing aid practice.

Then a hearing aid manufacturer offered me a loaded IBM laptop for free as a way of encouraging loyalty from my new company. All the years of striving and desiring a laptop ended in a gift from God.

## PORTAL TO HEAVEN

God chose to give me the very thing that I desired and needed by giving me something I hadn't asked for: a job which wrote integrity into my character.

If it ever upsets you that God isn't doing things your way, consider that you may be a character in the middle of His novel and He has not yet finished writing the chapter.

*'For my thoughts are not your thoughts, neither are your ways my ways,' declares the Lord. ... [I shall] accomplish what I please, and it shall prosper in the thing for which I sent it.*

**Isaiah 55:8, 11 (NIV). Editor's bracket.**

On November 22, 1963, C.S. Lewis drew his last breadth. I am thankful for Lewis because he surely knew that writing is at once a marathon, a sprint, a race and something in between.

Consider the magnitude within the brevity of the razor-sharp dagger Lewis uses to instantly kill the argument that Christ was merely a good man.

"I am trying here to prevent anyone saying the really foolish thing that people often say about Him: 'I'm ready to accept Jesus as a great moral teacher, but I don't accept his claim to be God.' That is the one thing we must not say. A man who was merely a man and said the sort of things Jesus said would not be a great moral teacher. He would either be a lunatic — on the level with the man who says he is a poached egg — or else he would be the Devil of Hell. You must make your choice. Either this man was, and is, the Son of God, or else a madman or something worse. You can shut him up for a fool, you can spit at him and kill him as a demon or you can fall at his feet and call him Lord and God, but let us not come with any patronizing nonsense about his being a great human teacher. He has not left that open to us. He did not intend to."

Because of that day's significance in American history, many were unaware that C.S. Lewis crossed his finish line on November 22, 1963. But when his feet hit the streets of gold there were crowds with well-wishers and plenty of bottles of living water.

## ꝒORTAL ꟾO ꞪEAVEN

Everyone has been given a pen of the heart. What is it writing?

*And the LORD answered me: 'Write the vision; make it plain on tablets, so he may run who reads it.'*

**Habakkuk 2:2 (ESV)**

Historically, Christians and Jews say a prayer of thanksgiving at different times of the day. The most repeated and well-known is "Grace" before meals.

Monasteries are known for pausing in the morning, noontime and evening to give thanks and praise to God. It's a consecration, a recognition that God is responsible for our day and is worthy of thanksgiving. Of course, monks are in the habit of Vespers which vary from order to order.

It is no surprise that there is scriptural basis for offering thanksgiving – especially at night.

The night is like prime real estate in terms of time for all manner of thanksgiving because it is when we are able to reflect on the incredible ways in which God has exhibited His faithfulness for this particular day.

Whether you use your smart phone, watch, home or office clock or are in the habit of noticing the sun at various places in the sky, the least this morning-noon-evening discipline can do is get your mind off problems and challenges. The best it can do is get you in the habit of being more aware of His presence and faithfulness.

## PORTAL TO HEAVEN

You may not feel led to wear a robe. Yet, what monks discovered long ago about the habit of thanksgiving is something that never goes out of style.

*It is good to give thanks to the Lord and to sing praises to Your name,*
*O Most High; to declare Your lovingkindness in the morning*
*and Your faithfulness by night...*

**Psalm 92:1,2 (NASB)**

**Also read: Psalm 55:17 (NIV)**

Scripture admonishes us to always be thankful, and that includes the times when we are in pain, dealing with frustration or in agony.

Life is not one-dimensional. Some things will be going well while other things will be going sour. That's just the way life will come at us.

Recently, a friend passed away in the same city where a relative was in labor at the exact same time. Death and life. Sorrow and joy.

So why would the scriptures command us to always be thankful? Moreover, even if there is sense behind that same exhortation, how do we get ourselves to the point where joy becomes a constant intrinsic state?

My answer comes from the gym. If you work out, your muscles get stronger and you are able to lift more.

If we work on developing thanksgiving on a daily basis, we will be able to lift the burdens of life with a sense of thankfulness.

Muscles don't come overnight. But it might lighten your load when you discover that it takes only 26 muscles to manage a smile versus 62 to create a frown.

## ᑭORTAL ᏀTO ᕼEAVEN

It may still feel like 26 reps, but that's a heck of a lot less than 62.

*Rejoice always, pray without ceasing, in everything give thanks;*
*for this is the will of God in Christ Jesus for you.*

**1 Thessalonians 5:16,17,18 (NKJV)**

With the strains of "O Little Town of Bethlehem"* making its way into my soul via ear buds, I am thrust into the Christmas season on the day after Thanksgiving.

While Thanksgiving is not on the biblical calendar, it seamlessly prepares us for Advent. For what could make "the dear Christ enter in" more than a meek and thankful heart?

And yet, just as there was a battle over the babe in Bethlehem, there is a more than a minor skirmish over every soul regarding Christmas. I don't have to look past my heart to feel the tension whether in relationships, finances, traveling, scheduling or memories.

Regarding the latter, everyone carries remembrances of Christmas-past as surely as Scrooge's first uninvited nighttime guest. Some are picture-perfect moments whose photos have become faded and ghostly because one or some in that same photograph are no longer with us. Others with photographic memories can recall every hurt of the holidays and so they carry a dread that makes them want to fast-forward their calendar to January.

## PORTAL TO HEAVEN

As "O Little Town of Bethlehem" completes its third stanza in my ears, I hear the greatest reason to be thankful: the reassurance that Christmas truly is a time when no soul needs to be alone. "No ear may hear His coming, but in this world of sin, where meek souls will receive him still, the dear Christ enters in."

*She will give birth to a son, and they will call him Immanuel, which means 'God is with us.'*

**Matthew 1:23 (NLT) Editor's emphasis.**

# PEN YOUR PORTALS

The week immediately after Thanksgiving is a bridge of sorts. It takes us into the Christmas season and gives us an on-deck type of feeling.

Some are ready for the holidays. Some are overwhelmed and don't know where or how to start. Others don't want to cross over into the yuletide until they are actually in the Christmas spirit.

Whether it's seasonal like going from Thanksgiving to Christmas or whether it's going one place to another, bridges safely bring us over troubled waters or deep ravines.

A speaker once suggested that there are stages to transitions or bridges. His research shows that we go through the following: 1) an ending where things shut down; 2) a desert where all is dry and there seems to be no promise, and 3) a breakthrough to a new beginning or destiny.

## PORTAL TO HEAVEN

During these times, Jesus himself is the bridge. We can only safely cross over when we know who it is that is strong enough to bear the weight of our life. Unfortunately, we may even need a bridge in a desert.

*But when God ... called me by his grace, was pleased to reveal his Son in me so that I might preach him among the Gentiles, my immediate response was not to consult any human being. I did not go up to Jerusalem to see those who were apostles before I was, but I went into Arabia. Later I returned to Damascus. Then after three years, I went up to Jerusalem.*

**Galatians 1:15-18a (NIV)**

In a figurative sense, bridges help us cross over from one side of life to another. Without them, we get stuck.

If there is fog ahead, does it mean that the bridge is not there or is it temporarily hidden?

I was in such a situation many years ago. I had used all of my money buying property on which to build a home. The bank declined to give me a loan for a modular house. They said I needed a bridge loan to buy the home and then they would lend me money to put it up. When I explained the predicament to my landlord, he said he would lend me the money. We went down to his bank. He withdrew the money. He became my bridge.

Unbeknownst to me, the bank had some closing fees at the end and I was $5,000 short. My brother bridged that gap for me with a loan.

In both circumstances, I didn't know I needed a bridge and I couldn't see a bridge ahead.

## ᏢORTAL ᏀTO ᎻEAVEN

There's a type of bridge called a truss bridge. God has built "trust bridges" at crucial moments in my life. He calls us to ride along and trust that somewhere in that fog there's a bridge.

*When you pass through the waters, I will be with you.*

**Isaiah 43:2 (NIV)**

Troubled water can come from sudden floods, long rainy seasons, winter runoffs, great storms, the merging of a few great rivers or bays, and steep declines that cause whitewater and waterfalls.

In life, troubled water can seem to come on any day for any reason or on the one day I forgot my life vest.

That's the very reason the beautiful strains of Art Garfunkel's vocals and Paul Simon's moving melody and lyrics in "Bridge Over Troubled Waters" soaked so many souls. It certainly packed biblical power.

The original two verses lean on imagery elicited from words and phrases like weary, feeling down, tears, when friends just can't be found, evening falls and pain. Oh, brother.

I don't know what was going on in Paul Simon's life when he wrote it, but it struck a chord throughout the world. And why? Because we all need a friend like that.

I've needed to be that friend and sometimes I wasn't. I needed others to be that friend and sometimes they were not.

## PORTAL TO HEAVEN

Jesus said we were His friends. So when others fail us, He's there. He also said we are to be like Him. So wouldn't it be nice if He could delegate that bridge construction to His crew and have all of us follow through?

*Greater love hath no man than this: that a man lay down his life for his friends.*

**John 15:13 (NIV)**

Bridges connect us to worlds of philosophy. The question becomes, "What specific river, bay or water body am I deliberately crossing over?"

For me, the answer was simple. I needed to cross over me. I was living for myself. The most interesting aspect of this gulf is that it got harder to recognize just how polluted my waters had become. I got used to my thoughts. I owned my philosophy. It became self-perpetuating.

The Word of God or scripture is a bridge that took me over the sewerage of self. As I began to study Proverbs and the life of Christ through the gospels, I actually woke up. I was like Rip Van Winkle. It took time to truly cross that bridge.

Jesus was a carpenter on earth. He knows how to build. While a bit mystical, Jesus and the Word of God are intertwined theologically. The Apostle John writes of Jesus as "the Word." While Jesus is not a paper bible and the words therein actually came after Him in a timeline sense, He is still the Word of God. The Word of God as scripture and our actual Savior are our bridge over self and sin.

## PORTAL TO HEAVEN

While wooden bridges seem a bit unreal today, Jesus used every splinter of a tree to help me "cross" over from my selfish, Rip-Van-Winkle state. The bridge is free because He paid the toll.

*And the Word was made flesh, and dwelt among us.*

**John 1:14 (KJV)**

The engineering students at my college had a senior project in which they were given a few sheets of white paper. They had to construct a bridge. The bridge that supported the most weight received an A+ and won the coveted first prize.

When I was frustrated about how slow my spiritual growth was going, my father-figure said I reminded him of a time when his commute slowed to a crawl due to road construction. His impatience with the length of the project began to get to him until God spoke very clearly as to why the crew had to go down so many layers beneath the pavement. "This road is being designed for heavy traffic," God said. It was a major commuting highway, not a side street.

That was a profound lesson. Many young people are launched into responsibilities prematurely due to their talent. But their character and/or stage in life just hasn't prepared them for such serious burdens. Yet.

## PORTAL TO HEAVEN

If engineering students can make a paper bridge that handles 1,047 pounds, how much more will the Project Manager of the Galaxies design our life's bridge to carry the weighty traffic for which we are built!

*I will not drive them out before you in a single year, that the land may not become desolate and the beasts of the field become too numerous for you. I will drive them out before you little by little, until you become fruitful and take possession of the land.*

**Exodus 23:29 (KJV)**

# PEN YOUR PORTALS

# December
## PORTALS
### To HEAVEN

No sacrilegious pun intended, but please don't throw the baby out with the bathwater this Christmas when it comes to your opinion of Saint Nicholas, the patron saint of children.

Nicholas was born into a wealthy family around 270 A.D. He was raised as a devout Christian when the present-day Turkey wasn't always friendly to his faith. He would eventually be exiled and incarcerated in a prison so filled with bishops, priests and deacons that there was no room for murderers, thieves and robbers.

When he died on December 6, 343 A.D., his relics were secured in Myra but later brought to Bari where they would be safe from invading Turks. In those days as today, relics attracted  pilgrims which had spiritual and financial implications for the host city.

## ᏢORTAL ᏟO ᎭEAVEN

Just as Nick was literally stolen from one city to another, his spirit of benevolence has ironically been the victim of thievery by those who dare to profit from a man who would even give a modern-day fake Santa the shirt off his back or stitch up the lady who was run over at the Black Friday sale at Walmart.

When kids, of whom Nicholas was so fond, think about Santa, it is doubtful that the vast majority of them are thinking about giving everything away like this great saint.  Nicholas, who saved so many children in his day, led a life of tribute to The Baby who had saved Nick himself.

*And she will have a son, and you are to name him Jesus, for he will save his people from their sins …*

**Matthew 1:21 (NLT)**
**Also read: Matthew 2:16 (NKJV)**

"It was the night before Christmas …"

This could be one of the most innocent, destructive poems ever penned. It is doubtful that the authors could have foreseen the damage that it did to Christmas.

Holidays always seem to be in the middle of a tug of war between Satan and Christians. Note how Hallow's Eve turned into the devil's day and the resurrection of Jesus has turned into a candy celebration ushered in by a hippity-hoppity chocolate bunny.

"Do you believe in Santa Claus?" is a much more used phrase than "Do you believe in Jesus Christ?"

When this subject is raised, indignation probably arises more than conviction to many followers of Jesus Christ.

## ᖇORTAL ᒍTO ᕼEAVEN

How could a fictitious fat man in a red suit squeeze out the Christ Child by simply getting Christians to rationalize that "it's all about giving?" If I had a time machine, I'd pick up Saint Nicholas in my sled and make our way to the house of the author of the freshly-written "Night Before Christmas," and I'd remind the poet of the true reason for the season.

*No one serving as a soldier gets entangled in civilian affairs, but rather tries to please his commanding officer… For false Christs and false prophets will appear and perform great signs and wonders that would deceive even the elect, if that were possible.*

**2 Timothy 2:4 (NIV), Matthew 24:24 (BSB)**

Words. I love them.

In the dictionary, words give the impression of neutrality. They are what they are and that is that.

But in the hands of a writer or anyone of influence, words can spin the world on its axis.

And that is exactly what happened when the innocent pen of Clement Moore crafted a poem that first appeared in the newspaper of my neighboring town of Troy, New York.

"A Visit from St. Nicholas" or "The Night Before Christmas" eventually became a famous poem that has now led to such classics as "Grandma Got Run Over Be A Reindeer" with words that might make Webster grimace. Songwriter Randy Brooks wrote: "She had hoof-prints on her forehead and incriminating Claus marks on her back."

I don't know whether Moore ever intended Santa to have reckless tendencies or that grandmothers should be caricaturized in such a manner, but that's exactly what words can do: get out of control and become a DWI of the pen.

## PORTAL TO HEAVEN

Jesus is the Word according to the Bible, and the minute you drift from that is when words, whether innocent and ignorant, become dangerous to cultures, generations, and yes, even grandmas.

*So the Word became human and made his home among us. He was full of unfailing love and faithfulness. And we have seen his glory, the glory of the Father's one and only Son.*

**John 1:14 (NLT)**

It's funny how we remember every detail of a wrong committed against us, but conveniently forget the many strands of grace and benevolence that we've been shown.

And yet, there are times when acts of kindness are such that neither individuals nor history forget them. These acts may even get passed on so long that their stories get embellished as time goes by.

Take into consideration that Saint Nicholas lived seventeen centuries ago in what is modern Turkey. It was a time when there were no reporters, newspapers or iPhones to instantaneously and forever record the actions of a day. There is the possibility that some of the stories of this great man have either been altered or, worse yet, forgotten.

With that in mind, we must guess that there have been an estimated 100 billion people who have come before us since his time. If this is so, why is someone like Nicholas remembered through the clutter of history? Surely, there were others who could have been the object of legend.

## PORTAL TO HEAVEN

Nicholas' generosity was so aligned with his Savior that the parallels could not be taken for granted or lost either in his time or through the birth of tens of billions of people during the following centuries.

And what of our lives? May our actions be so brilliant that wise men will see an unforgettable light as bright and long lasting as stars that are seen for millennia.

*Let your light so shine before men, that they may see your good works and glorify your Father in heaven.*

**Matthew 5:16 (NKJV)**
**Also read: Daniel 12:3 (NIV), Philippians 2:15b (NIV)**

While Saint Nicholas is widely known for spiritual and practical heroics in many areas, he was especially famous as the patron saint of children.

If half the stories of his kindness and generosity are true, you might say he had a lot of spiritual offspring. If ever there was a "Father Christmas," this was the guy.

The most famous story related to Nicholas is the one where by the cover of night he secretly threw gold coins through an open window so that the daughters of a poor man would have a dowry in order to get married. When some of the coins serendipitously landed in stockings that were perhaps drying over or near the fireplace, the girls had found a still-missing benefactor.

Although Nick has been lost to a caricature of his real self, what has cryptically survived is the mysterious man who looks after children.

So then, it is poetic justice that Nick is alligned with the holiday associated with a baby.

## ᖴORTAL ᏻTO ᖺEAVEN

The ironic twist of God on this entire plot: a heavenly child appears to look after mankind.

*This will be a sign to you: You will find a baby wrapped in cloths and lying in a manger… and a little child shall lead them… For God so loved the world that He gave His only begotten Son, that whoever believes in Him should not perish but have everlasting life.*

**Isaiah 11:16 (KJV), Luke 2:12 (NIV), John 3:16 (NKJV)**

The virgin birth of Jesus is as far-fetched a story as any author could dream. But God's poetic license is not revoked in this case, whether or not Joseph liked the script.

Mary's pregnancy is truly unbelievable. The only way it makes sense is to juxtapose it against God's Holy Spirit being born within us. The two are so far out that they only gel when intertwined. For what is stranger, a virgin birth or rebirth in us? Nicodemus certainly scratched his head.

Advent is a time to ponder the wonder of a God who impregnates a world with the unbelievable: that we could be the offspring of His goodness. Many men and women would do what Joseph tried to do: put such a dream away because it's the ultimate impossible dream. And it took a dream to help Joseph realize that God is a pretty big dreamer.

We don't know when Joseph died, but he ended up living the dream – every day of the year. We have this same opportunity.

## PORTAL TO HEAVEN

This nativity story's end result is that we lay hold of the unbelievable; that is, "Emmanuel," meaning "God with us." It's poetic license to the extreme and yet I'm a captive to this script.

*Behold, a virgin shall be with child, and shall bring forth a son, and they shall call his name Emmanuel, which being interpreted is, God with us... In the beginning was the Word, and the Word was with God, and the Word was God.*

**Matthew 1:23 (KJV), John 1:1 (NIV)**

Life is enlarged by figurative unexpected pregnancies...

People are genuinely drawn to Jesus during the season of Advent – the month preceding Christmas.

More than just holiday lights are illuminated at this time. Individuals seem to have revelations and God often uses this month to set up a rebirth of Jesus in many of us.

And so it was with the earthly father of Jesus. When Joseph found out that Mary was pregnant, he immediately wanted to back out of the deal. In his mind, it wasn't the way God should work. Moreover, he didn't expect God to specifically work through someone so close to him.

## PORTAL TO HEAVEN

Recognize and embrace the specific people that God uses to birth Jesus in all of us. These unexpected pregnancies enlarge us. At this time of year when emotions seem to get jostled around by the season, we are called to pay attention to what those feelings are and who they are directed to, and that can help us unwrap the presence of Jesus.

*... for the Child who has been conceived in her is of the Holy Spirit...*

**Matthew 1:20b (KJV)**

The Christmas season is pregnant with possibilities. This is vividly paralleled in the account of Mary's expectations.

It's in this very season that He offers me the unexpected through my own expectations. If I am eager for Him to impregnate my heart with a clearer vision of the Christ child, I will undoubtedly find Him in the stables of life. But only after a pilgrimage of faith.

My first step is to be deliberate about following His star. How could I find the Baby without some specific direction?

Heaven's very pregnancy is within me. The wise men and Mary were both expecting. When I earnestly ask God about the Christmas season, my expectant heart is met with unexpected joy in unsuspected people, places and circumstances.

Along this path, I may be met with some deception by some ruler trying to supplant Him. This seems rather plausible today. I may not arrive on the day of His birth. I may need to caravan with others who see what I see. I may have to bring my finest gifts.

## PORTAL TO HEAVEN

Getting to the place where my expectations are met with the unexpected is the foretaste of heaven that Mary's pregnancy delivers. For those willing to travel Advent's dusty roads, it truly is a season of wonder.

In the end, this pregnancy delivers us.

*We have seen His star in the East and have come to worship Him.*

**Matthew 2:2b (NAS)**

It's good to ask God for His presence throughout the season instead of focusing on one day. This is an old lesson that needs to be relearned. When I began intentionally viewing the holidays as a season of a few months, it took off a lot of the pressure of Christmas week and, specifically, Christmas Day.

Everyone and every family has a stream of life and this tends to flow through the lives of relatives, their faith community and a region. Within those relations, there are usually treasures to be presented to the Child of Christmas.

By divvying up the greater season, I can bring my gifts to the King. In some circumstances, I have to saddle up my camel and get to New Jersey, Pennsylvania or California. At other times, the Babe is as close as my wife.

## ᏢORTAL ᏯO ᏨEAVEN

See holiday season spread over a few months and pray that Christmas Day spills over into 365 days. Perhaps this determination and deliberation will overflow onto my calendar year and portend an eternal yearning culminating with eventually seeing the face of Christ in others every day.

*No one has seen God at any time; if we love one another, God abides in us, and His love is perfected in us.*

**1 John 4:12 (NKJV)**

Caroling can be viewed in a sacred or secular light.

For many years, we caroled in our neighborhood the week before Christmas. This could have gotten tedious after 20 years, but it never did because the holidays and worship were and are times for heavenly visitations.

One of our first stops was at the home of my German neighbor, Oolie. He would invite us in and sit down at his piano and play "Stille Nacht" ("Silent Night") and only in the key of C. He followed this up with a German sweet for all of us. His excitement to see us and play along is still one of those Christmas treasures in my memory bank.

Behind our house was a farm that housed long wooden wagons, carriages and the Clydesdales. One year I made the financial plunge to hire one. When the night arrived, so did the North Pole.

However, the fierce winds and record-setting wind chills of 30-below didn't stop twenty of us from singing our hearts out. We drove a station wagon behind so the carolers could jump in the car every few minutes to warm up. We popped in a restaurant and shocked diners who wondered what manner of people would do this in such inclement weather.

## ₧ORTAL ꙅTO ꜣEAVEN

Caroling is worship and God always welcomes us when He is adored. Just ask the shepherds, the wise men and those who seek him today.

*Boldly and freely he proclaimed the kingdom of God and taught about the Lord Jesus Christ.*

**Acts 28:31 (NAS)**

# PEN YOUR PORTALS

I tried not to glance at my front yard every time I came up my driveway. In the center was an inverted aquamarine baby pool that I had strategically positioned over a huge pile of raked leaves to keep them from blowing away.

One week went by, two weeks, then six weeks. It wasn't a matter of procrastination. I had two mowers down coupled with an upcoming deadline. When I had the time, the mowers weren't working. When I had the mowers, I had no time.

Though the pile of leaves was only a few feet high, it seemed as high as a mountain.

Finally, my deadline passed and I was a free man. However, snow was predicted for the next day. I went to bed bemoaning that this defeat would haunt me through the winter and that the spring cleanup would be a bear.

When I awoke, the pile disappeared. Literally.

A Christmastime blanket of snow graced my front yard and erased my guilt. Just like that, this gigantic failure and its accompanying shame had been replaced with a makeover that no reality show could match.

## PORTAL TO HEAVEN

This portrait of purity of the color white was the complete and instantaneous metaphor for the forgiveness of sin. Grace had painted the grounds and made the imperfection vanish.

*'Come now, let us settle the matter,' says the Lord. 'Though your sins are like scarlet, they shall be as white as snow; though they are red as crimson, they shall be like wool.'*

**Isaiah 1:18 (NIV)**

I have a near life-size manger that is sitting behind my garage. Unintentionally, it's become a metaphor of how public displays of Christmas are getting tucked away.

Christmas greetings have gotten tucked away as well. "Merry Christmas" has been supplanted by "Season's Greetings" or "Happy Holidays."

The only thing left is our thought life. Is it possible that thinking could join displays and greetings in the junkyard of the quieting of Christmas?

Consider the last time you heard people in a mall or by the office water cooler talking about the incarnation and magnificence of God breaking heaven's silence. Jesus does not deserve silence in return for such an act.

Yet I ask myself, "Have I quieted Christmas?" I think on conversations where I've impotently asked, "So, what did you get the kids?" or "Where are you headed for the holidays?" or the heady "You think it's going to be a white Christmas?"

## PORTAL TO HEAVEN

Realize that either society influences us or we influence the culture. The manger went out to the edge of my yard where everyone can see the Baby who makes angels exclaim, "Glory to God in the highest, and on earth peace, goodwill toward men!"

*After seeing him, the shepherds told everyone what had happened and what the angel had said to them about this child. All who heard the shepherds' story were astonished... The shepherds went back to their flocks, glorifying and praising God for all they had heard and seen.*

**Luke 2:17-20 (NLT)**

Clearly, Handel's "Messiah" broke through during its use as a fundraiser, most famously for a children's home in London called the Foundling Hospital.

He could not have written this passionate piece without being moved by something far more than English currency.

The prime example lies in the humorous or sacrilegious substitution, "Surely He has worn our griefs" for "Surely He has borne our briefs".

Could it have been that this very line that so acutely captured the hardship of those in the Foundling Home was the very thing responsible for elevating the oratorio to a must-see status in 1750? As outstanding as the music was, could Handel's revelation of Christ's identification with the poor be what moved a king and the privileged class to their feet – and their pocketbooks?

Handel declared that he "saw heaven opened and the great God himself" while writing the famous chorus. Evidently, Handel learned heaven's lesson. For how else could he have written the timeless masterpiece in just 24 days?

## PORTAL TO HEAVEN

The best art is created when an artist puts himself in a position to borrow from heaven and lend it to earth.

*I saw the Lord sitting on a throne, high and lifted up, and the train of His robe filled the temple... seraphim cried to one another and said, 'Holy, holy, holy is the Lord of hosts; The whole earth is full of His glory!' Also I heard the voice of the Lord, saying: 'Whom shall I send, and who will go for Us?' Then I said, 'Here am I! Send me.'*

**Isaiah 6:1b,2,3,8 (NKJV)**

While King George III may have had some problems with the brewing rebellion across the pond in America, the monarch had no trouble recognizing the divine inspiration of "Messiah." He was so moved during the "Hallelujah Chorus" that he stood to his feet. It was the custom for people to follow suit and to this day audiences rise during the chorus.

Or do they? In a New York City performance, the man next to me sat during the Hallelujah Chorus. This is becoming more common. The irony cannot be lost that dissidents in the third row pay top dollar to listen to some of Messiah's opening lines: "But who can endure the day of His coming? And who can stand when He appears?"

## PORTAL TO HEAVEN

Within the lyrics from *Messiah*, judgment and mercy are always offered by Jesus. In King George's time, a rebel would pay with his life. My concern for the sitters is that they will face that same consequence if they ignore the warning from where they sit in the third row. Even so, there is still time, for the Lord always stands ready to receive the repentant sinner.

*'Return to Me, and I will return to you,' says the Lord of hosts.*

**Malachi 3:7. (ESV)**

**Also read: Malachi 3:2b (ESV)**

As a refresher, you may recall that magi, or wise men, came from the east to find where the king of the Jews had been born.

Naturally, their first stop was King Herod's palace where they asked him about the whereabouts of the Christ.

Perhaps you'll remember that Herod feigns a desire to worship the newborn king and sends them to Bethlehem with instructions to bring word back as to the exact whereabouts of the baby.

The king is jealous that another king would dethrone him.

But Herod loses track of the magi who are warned in a dream not to return to him. The king is furious and sends his henchmen to find and kill the baby.

Most of us think of the "slaughter of the innocents" in Bethlehem as the cruelest and most wicked act imaginable. We think, "How could he have done this?"

## PORTAL TO HEAVEN

We have all tried to kill off thoughts and actions that would dethrone us - and not as a one-time deal, but on a daily basis.

Out of all of the refresher courses about Christmas and the millions of subplots surrounding the birth of Jesus Christ, it would do us well to remember this lesson above them all because it seems to be the most convenient and easiest to forget.

*Then Jesus said to His disciples, 'If anyone wishes to come after Me, he must deny himself, and take up his cross and follow Me.'*

**Matthew 16:24 (ESV)**
**\*"O, Little Town of Bethlehem" by Brooks & Redner.**

# PEN YOUR PORTALS

For my siblings' present one year, I converted what was originally Brownie-camera film from the 1950s and 1960s from VHS to DVD.

This included some Christmas footage. And like Luke's gospel introduction, I'd like to set out an orderly account of our holiday. It occurred 5,717 miles west of Bethlehem, Israel. The angels would have found me in North Plainfield, New Jersey.

What stand out in these home movies were the smiles. If it weren't for these films, I wouldn't even recall what presents were given to us. Yet with or without the help of the Brownie-camera footage, I can recall like it was yesterday the excitement of decorating the Christmas tree.

I'd make a painstaking effort of placing the individual thin strips of tinsel so they'd look like shiny icicles. After an hour or two, this would get a bit tedious. I would then cheat and throw a dozen or more on and just spread them around a bit. The static electricity from the ones that were dropped on the rug and under the radiator made them a bit stubborn to clean up.

Our family and friends were some of the obvious treasures that the films revealed. They didn't come by camels, but their cars certainly filled up our semi-circular driveway.

## PORTAL TO HEAVEN

Jesus was the invisible visitor who never failed to show up in the starring role in our home movies.

*The Son is the image of the invisible God, the firstborn over all creation.*

**Colossians 1:15 (NIV)**

If we're smart, we'll love what our parents cherish. My mom loved Perry Como and Andy Williams and all the crooners who made Christmas come alive through their voices.

I'll never forget "Christmas In Italy," an album that featured a variety of styles in their native tongue. I still listen to it during the holidays. I loved the children's choir. A particular favorite cut was one that started with "Ding, dong, dong." Now, that I understood. It was as if Christmas was ringing our doorbell.

When we hold fast to the traditions that our parents loved because they were holding tight to what our Savior loved, we do more than just honor them. We covenant to keep their hearts beating in ours.

Mom knew that the strains of Christmas music that began in the cool air over some shepherds 2,000 years ago must never be turned off.

Charlie Brown's friend Linus had it right, as well: "Glory to God in the highest, and on earth peace, goodwill toward men."

## PORTAL TO HEAVEN

It compels us to carol. In a sense, we then join the multitudes of heaven who know the words to that "Gloria" so well.

*And suddenly there was with the angel a multitude of the heavenly host praising God...*

**Luke 2:13 (NIV)**

I grew up in an Italian-American family and the importance of food upon on our memory banks – especially at Christmas – cannot be underestimated.

Mom's kitchen was like a basement boiler that kept everything warm. This was Lucy's "apron countenance."

My sister Lucille recently recalled the fried dough with just enough tomato sauce and the turkey and lasagna. (This was while we were grating fresh Polly-O mozzarella for her own magical lasagna. The legend lives on!)

But kitchens transition to tables, and it was around the dining room that forks, knives and napkins replaced aprons. The fruit of Mom's labor was a meal that morphed into conversations and back to food again that Italians know so well.

The table was set for the nine of us, and we will never forget the aroma and tastes that somehow matched our anticipation. We all had assigned seats. This made us feel like we had a literal special place in our family.

Perhaps Mom's greater legacy was that she invited others to join us. When something smells that good, it is easy to imagine why they accepted.

## PORTAL TO HEAVEN

Another family – those who have accepted Christ's aromatic invitation to join Him – will sit down around a feast that will exceed all expectations. But I must say, our house did get a sneak preview – especially at Christmas.

*Many get invited; only a few make it [accept it].*

**Matthew 22:14 (The Message). Editor's addition.**

Through the eyes of a child...

When we were young, one of the coolest things was staying up late on Christmas Eve and the sacred feel of going to Midnight Mass. The church was standing-room-only and that meant it easily outpolled any hotspot or bar in town.

If you didn't get to church early enough, you were doomed to stand in the back near the vestibule. Every time the door opened, we'd get a middle-of-the-night chill that would serve as a reminder to get there sooner next year.

I can't remember any sermons per se. But the Roman Catholic Church does a wonderful job with symbols. Little kids do well with these.

St. Joseph's Church in North Plainfield, New Jersey, had a crèche that would have made St. Francis proud.

Kneeling before the manger with its life-size Baby, I can recall that His porcelain face seemed to be looking right at me. I now realize that I had to be staring at him in order to understand his returned gaze from those beautiful eyes. It took years before I realized the profundity and accuracy of this interchange.

## PORTAL TO HEAVEN

It's amazing how close and low I was able to get to the Baby. It wasn't only because I was so young. It was because I was kneeling. This is what was birthed at Christmas through the eyes of a child.

*Let us kneel before the Lord our Maker...Draw near to God, and he will draw near to you.*

**Psalm 95:6 (NIV), James 4:8 (ESV)**

Saving the best for last...

One Christmas, my daughter Angelique asked for a bicycle. It was to be a 24-inch bike that would be just right for her size.

However, it had been another lean year and I didn't think I could swing the purchase. Angelique said she would understand if we couldn't afford the present. To say that broke my heart was an understatement.

God decided to swing it for me. I was in another town and by chance I stopped at a store that just happened to have a purple girl's 24-inch bike on sale. I still don't remember how I fit it into the car, but I do recall thanking God every mile on my way home!

On Christmas morning, we opened every present and Angelique never complained or showed disappointment. But when I wheeled out her bike at the very last second, she broke into tears and it is still recorded in my memory as one of the best Christmas morning surprises because the best was saved for last.

## PORTAL TO HEAVEN

The first Christmas was so full of surprises that we should expect nothing less at the second coming of Christ. May you wake up on Christmas Day and every day and be filled the anticipation of the "Desire of the Nations."

*Arise, shine; For your light has come! And the glory of the Lord is risen upon you. For behold, the darkness shall cover the earth, And deep darkness the people; But the Lord will arise over you, And His glory will be seen upon you.*

**Isaiah 60:1,2 (NAS)**
**Also read: Act 1:11b**

# PEN YOUR PORTALS

"Honk, honk!" It's not a rude New York City cab driver.

It's the "horns" of the Canadian geese overhead stopping you in your tracks.

"How do they find their way back home?" you ask yourself.

There is an analogy here to time. How does a human know where he is going with his life? We set out on a path that lands us on the doorstep of death. It's innate. But what about the in-between time?

Everything hinges on our definition of the who, what, why, where and how of home – and not so much the when.

What is my intrinsic desire/driver and where is that taking me? I really don't like driving behind a bumper sticker that teases, "Life is hard. Then you die."

I want to go somewhere. I want to go home.

## PORTAL TO HEAVEN

As with the instinct of migratory birds, eternity is so built into the human soul that it is our wings. If we're standing still, lost or going in the wrong direction, perhaps it's not a rude intrusion when we hear a honk.

*I came forth from the Father and have come into the world; I am leaving the world again and going to the Father… And this is the way to have eternal life – to know you, the only true God, and Jesus Christ, the one you sent to earth.*

**John 16:28 (NASB), John 17:3 (NLT)**

I briefly met a saleswoman at a modular home sales park. She invited me to take a self-guided tour through the models. That was like taking one of those historic house or garden tours … yeah, right.

You have to forget that you are in a parking lot made up of gravel and tar and homes propped up on cement blocks. Ah, but once inside, the magic begins.

It's amazing to see what architects can do with layout produced off a basic rectangular shape. Some have columns in the entrance, some have L-shaped kitchen-to-dining-to-living rooms, others have spa-like whirlpools in the middle of a gigantic bathroom, some have mudrooms so nice that you wouldn't want to get any mud in there and others have walk-in closets that are bigger than many houses I've seen in developing countries.

It's analogous to us. Modulars are all crafted to make you feel at home. They go way beyond the basics. Modular parks are meant to spark a desire in us to settle in - exactly what souls are designed to do.

## PORTAL TO HEAVEN

The characteristics we allow the Holy Spirit to build into us in increasing measure will determine the degree with which our "guests" will want to visit or even stay. Even if it's a brief encounter with a modular home saleswoman, will we be able to turn the table on her and make her feel at home?

*Make every effort to add to your faith goodness; and to goodness, knowledge; and to knowledge, self-control; and to self-control, perseverance; and to perseverance, godliness; and to godliness, mutual affection; and to mutual affection, love.*

**2 Peter 1:5-7 (NIV)**

Where is home? We wonder where we should settle down or which neighborhood to pick or even ponder whether weather should be the decisive factor in where we should make our home.

In biblical times, the common thread that wove the tents and lives of the patriarchs Abraham, Isaac and Jacob and many of their descendants was that these nomads allowed God to be their home. That's a wild and nebulous concept for westerners.

The story of Roman Catholic priest Father Kapaun is one of someone who knew that his home was where he was in the present; that God stakes out our address in the needs in front of us. In his case, it was what was in the "front" of him that he called home.

He left his boyhood home of Kansas and was determined as a chaplain to be used in the service of the military – whether that meant being bounced around in a Jeep in India, caring for soldiers' needs in Japan or being shipped out to the Korean conflict and walking a death-march to a prison camp in North Korea.

He was at home carrying sick and dying men and encouraging others to do the same. He resided with God in the breaking of the bread and sharing his last piece of bread with a diseased and disheartened fellow prisoner of war.

## PORTAL TO HEAVEN

God's permanent residence is often on the road of life.

*Instead, they were longing for a better country – a heavenly one. Therefore God is not ashamed to be called their God, for he has prepared a city for them.*

**Hebrews 11:6 (NIV)**

In elementary school, one of the nuns red-inked one of my true-false questions. I was a bit perplexed because I was sure my answer was correct. The question read: *We are on this earth for a long time: True__False__.*

Naturally, as an eight year-old, I answered "TRUE." That red ink was the kindest of corrections.

From Walt Disney's cryogenically frozen body and urban legends of Elvis sightings, it appears that even adults struggle with third-grade religion test answers.

St. Peter called his body a tent. Even well-made tents tend to have a shelf life or at least imply something of temporary quarters. Old St. Pete was used to seeing nomadic folks wandering around the Middle East. Moreover, The Rock saw the Alpha and Omega tread on the earth for a mere three years.

Having worked in the healthcare field for a good portion of my life, I have almost revered technological breakthroughs that are responsible for quality-of-life boosts and life-extending measures even to the minimizing of prayer, healing and the sovereignty of God.

## ᴘORTAL ᴛO ᴴEAVEN

The moment that we lean on concrete, timber and even temporary tents is when we repeat the mistake that I made when I was eight.

---

*I think it is right to refresh your memory as long as I live in the tent of this body, because I know that I will soon put it aside, as our Lord Jesus Christ has made clear to me. And I will make every effort to see that after my departure you will always be able to remember these things.*

**2 Peter 1:13-15 (NIV)**

I grew up in a 15-room New Jersey Victorian that seemed a little like "There Was an Old Woman Who Lived in a Shoe" in that there were seven kids and all of our friends. There was life and drama and two snoring parents in front of the television who nightly succumbed to exhaustion after howling at Archie Bunker's latest stereotype.

The towering octagonal witch's hat, the long stairway bannisters that we used to slide down, the wrap-around porch where we spent so many summer evenings eating the choicest of Italian delicacies, the third-floor balcony that put the entire neighborhood at our feet, the creepy servant's stairway off the kitchen, the 24-hour pool table and the red barn in the back were all part of this Victorian shoe that fit my mother quite well.

I went back home many years later and the only sound I heard was the creaking of the sagging porch stairs under my feet as I nervously approached the doorbell. The front door that my dad had stripped had weathered, the spindles were broken and rotted in a few places and the blue paint on the porch ceiling was peeling. The barn was gone and so were the many faces of all of us who ate at Mom's table. It was fitting that no one was home. Whoever lived there purchased architecture which, like a lot of the material world, is not something you can maintain forever.

## PORTAL TO HEAVEN

It is easy to mistake houses for homes. Each and every second, our choices buy us earthly real estate or a home made in heaven. The kid in me believes with all his heart that heaven's homes have the longest bannisters.

*Live in me. Make your home in me just as I do in you… Things that are seen don't last forever, but things that are not seen are eternal. That's why we keep our minds on the things that cannot be seen.*

**John 15:4 (The Message), 2 Corinthians 4:18 (CEV)**

# RESOURCES

**MOBILEGOD APP:**
*An incredibly powerful app that includes the Portals to Heaven blog and an intuitive twice-daily scripture-ping to your phone based on a survey you fill out. Also carries the phenomenal teaching of Back to The Bible.*

**SONRISEN.COM ("AWAKEN")**
*is an online devotional site and features the Portals to Heaven blog along with contributions from other guest writers and ministries.*

***THE KING'S FAVORITE BOOK STORYJOURNAL™** is an allegorical short story that inspires and teaches about the God who knows your struggles. Recommended for those who want to journal with God. Available in hardcover, faux leather and gift book. If coffee is part of your devotional and/or journaling process, we have customized King's Favorite mugs with Father-heart scriptures.*

**LIKE FATHER, LIKE SON**
*is a short novel and simple parable that sheds light on Christ as a Son and The Father's devotion to Him.*

***GAMALIEL'S ADVICE***
*is a novel based on the true story of The Mt. Soledad Cross in San Diego. The story and the screenplay written for about it weave a metaphorical tale about a World War II grandfather and his granddaughter which symbolizes their generational differences.*

**No Reputation Communications, LLC.**
**Norepcom@gmail.com**
**Booking & Ordering: 1-844-434-3277**
**Sonrisen.com | robertlacosta.com**

**I Want To Be Part of a Miracle**

**He Stood For Me**

**I Want to Hear**

**365
Does That Make
Today Christmas Day?**

**My Day Will Be My Act of Worship**

**The King's Favorite Book - Mugs**
Boston Irish Coffee Mug™. Mug Size:
3.3125"w x 4.25"h.

# ABOUT THE AUTHOR

## Beloved Blogger: "The Metaphor-Man."

Robert J. LaCosta has been writing for years about "portals to heaven" through metaphor, allegory and symbolism in his longstanding "Beloved Blogger" blog (robertlacosta.com)

He loves the presence of God through the many clues, cues and hints that God drops on a daily basis. He enjoys his annual journey through The Bible, The Old Testament and mining the treasures of Jesus. His passion is that of an investigative journalist out to expose the incredible love of The Trinity in the hope that readers become heaven-minded.

Photograph by Patrick Renzi

In addition to his books, LaCosta has penned over 2,000 songs and continues to write his monthly, "Retiring Retirement" column.

He loves speaking to groups and churches and those who want to learn about hearing from God.

He is the former C.E.O. of Hear For You, a large hearing aid and audiology practice. Part of his infinity for hearing God grew out of his extensive experience in natural hearing matters. He considers it a privilege to serve the hearing impaired and particularly senior citizens.

He deeply loves his family, extended family and friends, his local church, the wider Body of Christ, the regional community at large and he greatly appreciates his readers.

Made in the USA
San Bernardino, CA
08 December 2018